THE LIMITLESS REAL ESTATE LEADER

Building a Successful Business, Family, and Legacy

by Brenda A. Fontaine

Brenda A. Fontaine
The Limitless Real Estate Leader
Building a Successful Business, Family, and Legacy

Edited by: David Salter and Mary Lou Reynolds
Cover and interior design: Dan Yeager, Nu-Image Design

Library of Congress Control Number: 2016919320
ISBN: 978-0-9982876-0-7

Printed in the United States of America

PRAISE FOR
THE LIMITLESS
REAL ESTATE LEADER

"Brenda Fontaine is an industry superstar and for good reason! She leads as she lives with honesty, enthusiasm, and passion for building solid relationships for the long term. Read this book and heed its solid, practical advice. Success, after all isn't an accident. It's a practice anyone can learn and enjoy."

Brenda Garrand, CEO Garrand Partners, Portland, Maine

"I just read The Limitless Real Estate Leader and was riveted until I finished. I believe that through Brenda's open candid account of 1st her background, and then the steps that she took on her real estate journey, should be a beacon of light to anyone in any industry. You will glean wisdom and courage through reading this book."

-Dottie Bowe, Operating Principal of
Keller Williams Greater Portland Maine

"As a real estate investor I can attest to the fact that self-limiting beliefs can be your worst enemy. Thoughts become things and Brenda's book provides the blueprint to align your thought patterns with your vision and goals."

-Adam Todd, Real Estate Investor and Coach

"Brenda A. Fontaine has written a must-read resource for anyone wanting to break through to new levels of success. Read this book and learn from one of the best."

John Brubaker, Award-Winning Author, Speaker and Executive Coach

"This book spoke to me on three levels: as a realtor, father, and as a husband." You owe it to yourself to pick up a copy."

–Nate Wadsworth, Real Estate Investor and Representative: Maine House of Representatives

"As the owner of a family business I can tell you Brenda's book will help you amplify your results at the office and at home."

– Derek Volk, Author and President Volk Packaging

"This book is a must read for anyone in real estate, direct sales, or that has a dream deep down to want

to make that dream a reality. Brenda Fontaine has hit a home run on how to be limitless in one's mindset to achieve the real meaning of success in life and business."

-Tricia Adreassen, Media Personality, President and Founder of
Creative Publishing and Learning Institute, #1 Best Selling Author

"As a repeat customer of The Fontaine Team, I was excited to learn more about the lady behind the 'Fontaine' sign. The Limitless Real Estate Leader is educational and inspirational. As a fellow family business owner in Auburn, Maine, I've taken her lessons to heart and I know countless others will as well."

-Lori Gile, Controller and Owner, Auburn Concrete

"The Limitless Real Estate Leader will inspire you and give you valuable insight into Brenda's success. I took my business to the next level. If you read this book and take the action steps, you'll make it happen, just like Brenda did."

-Chad Sylvester, Broker/Owner Androvise Realty, Fontaine Family Team member (2011-2015)

"Brenda's wisdom transcends real estate. Leaders in any industry can benefit from her insights."

-Tim Worden, Former Broker/Owner Worden Realty, Licensed with Berkshire Hathaway

TABLE OF CONTENTS

Praise For The Limitless Real Estate Leader iii

Foreword ix

Dedication xiii

Acknowledgements xv

Introduction.. 3

Chapter 1: What I Learned from Mom and Dad 7

Chapter 2: Getting Started 21

Chapter 3: The Family Business 35

Chapter 4: Leadership is Like Being a Good Mother 61

Chapter 5: The Team Makes a Move 75

Chapter 6: It's All about the Client 93

Chapter 7: Reflections 109

Final Thoughts 119

Brenda's Success Tips 123

Brenda's Top Distinctions of a Superstar Sales Professional........ 127

Brenda's Family Business Rules 129

The Fontaine Difference 133

Fontaine Business Model 135

About the Author 139

FOREWORD

Brenda Fontaine has written a breakthrough book on business success. I can attest to the fact that the title *The Limitless Real Estate Leader* is very appropriate. As you're about to learn, Brenda embodies the term limitless, both personally and professionally.

I've known Brenda, her family, and her team for over a decade. First as neighbors, then as friends and colleagues. It has been a synergistic relationship and I consider myself fortunate to know Brenda and her team. In 2012 she hired me to speak to her company and my experience with them immediately made me think one thing... *When the day comes to sell my home, there isn't another person I'd trust more*.

That day came in April of 2016, and my experience as a client of the Fontaine Family Team confirmed, every step of the way, exactly what I knew about them. They don't sell houses – they help people find the right homes. There's a big difference; the former is a mere transaction, while the latter is a relationship based on caring about their clients. And they do it as a team: From start to finish, there were no disconnects, no false starts, no miscommunications – which is remarkable in any industry. One of the most admirable qualities she has engrained in her team is their collective vision. The team sees possibilities, not obstacles, and opportunities, not challenges. As a result, they have an amazing reputation.

During my 23-year career as a coach to executives and athletes, the biggest challenge I've seen that holds individuals, teams, and companies back is self-imposed limits. Too often people make the mistake of thinking that physical barriers like limited financial resources, poor facilities, or lack of personnel are what's holding back their success. In reality, for most people it's the mental baggage – all of the junk we carry around in our minds. Our thoughts, beliefs and ideas sabotage our performance by creating self-imposed limits on our potential. I call this saboteur the inner critic. I think everyone has an inner critic inside their head. Your inner critic is that little voice that talks to you and criticizes you.

Your inner critic says things to you like: *"You're not good enough. Other people are more qualified. You're not ready for that yet. What if you fail and you can't do it?"* Thoughts and comments like that drag down your performance by creating self-imposed limits.

Imagine carrying a cinder block around with you all day. (An 8"x8"x16" cinder block weighs exactly 39 lbs.) How productive and efficient would you be lugging that around? What would you say if I told you that you already are? This is the same emotional weight we carry in the form of mental blocks that limit our performance. Psychologist Aaron Beck actually determined that an inner critic's self-deprecatory comments are a root cause of depression in people.

It's very apropos that Brenda Fontaine asked me to write the foreword to *The Limitless Real Estate Leader*. In 2012 when I spoke to Brenda's organization, one of the points I made was the importance of how we talk to ourselves. Before you dive into reading her book, I want to take you through the same exercise I had Brenda's team do and have all my audiences do when I speak on mindset. Okay, ready?

Raise your hand if you have a little voice in your head that talks to you. Most people usually raise their hands but a select few don't. In their minds, they're saying to themselves, "I don't have a little voice inside my head." Perhaps you are one of the select few; if so, that's the very voice I'm speaking of!

Next:

1. I want you to stand up and do your very best to raise your right arm over your head as high as you can and keep it there.

2. Now I want you to reach a little higher.

3. Okay, take a look at how high your arm is now compared to when you first raised it.

(You can put your arm down now.)

How did you do? Was there a difference between 1 and 2 for you? Almost everyone reports that they are able to reach a little higher the second time. If that includes you, don't feel bad – it happens to almost everyone. Something stopped you the first time, right? There was no external barrier; the only barrier was internal. It was your inner critic creating a self-imposed limit when you raised your arm the first time.

Weren't my first instructions pretty specific? I asked you to do your best to raise your right arm as high as possible. The bottom line is that we all have an inner critic and nine times out of ten our inner critic doesn't serve us well. Your inner critic is usually wrong and it lies. Your inner critic's dialogue is merely limiting thoughts, thoughts you choose to believe. If you believe the thoughts of your inner critic, those mental blocks you're accumulating will become stumbling blocks or, worse yet, a wall.

Brenda's book is going to help you remove the self-imposed limits in your business and your life. How do I know? Because as you're about to read, it's precisely what Brenda has done. She removed and replaced the limiting thoughts that got programmed into her head during her formative years. She's going to teach you that being limitless isn't being fearless – it's taking action towards your goals in spite of your fears. And she leads by example; you'll learn the "how to" steps from her experiences she very candidly shares.

Lastly, don't let the real estate stories mislead you into thinking these ideas apply only to that industry. The fundamentals of becoming a limitless leader are precisely that – fundamental – because they transcend all industries. It's a real nuts-and-bolts book that will challenge you and your team to reach higher. In fact, after I read it I found myself re-examining my professional goals to make sure I wasn't setting limits on my performance.

Enjoy reading *The Limitless Real Estate Leader.* I know I did!

Best,

John Brubaker
Award-Winning Author, Speaker, Coach
CoachBru.com

DEDICATION

I dedicate this book to my grandchildren Makaela, Dustin, Ridge, Bree, and Brock.

You have brought so much joy into my life. My wish for you is the best life ever filled with an abundance of happiness. But my wishing it for you will not make it happen. You must make the right choices.

Follow your dream – and dream big! Write your dreams down because they become your goals.

Stay positive even when it's hard. Keep your word – trust is everything. Forgive everyone – including yourself. Stop worrying – it's such a waste of time. Push through your fears – one baby step at a time. Be grateful every day – when you look for blessings, you find them everywhere. Grateful people are happy people. Choose wisely. The choices you make today will affect your future and also the future of your children and grandchildren.

This is your life, and you have limitless potential and limitless opportunities. Believe in yourself – you are unstoppable! I will be with you every step of the way, cheering you on and smiling with pride.

ACKNOWLEDGEMENTS

This book would not be possible without the help of some very important people.

To my friend, coach, and advisor, John Brubaker: If you would not have moved into our neighborhood and become a friend and business advisor, this book may never have happened. Your advice, encouragement, and connections made this all possible, and I thank you.

To my editor, David Salter: Thank you for your encouragement. I appreciate your knowledge and expertise in making my book the best it can be.

To my book designer, Dan Yeager: Thank you for always answering my endless questions so promptly. You are extremely talented.   I'm very fortunate to have had you work on this project.

To my typist, Peggy Foster: You were the first to read my chapters. Your feedback encouraged me to keep going. I feel very blessed that our paths crossed and that you agreed to help me.

Thank you to my family – my daughters, Melissa, Angie, and Crystal and sons-in-law, Bill, Clayton and Tim: Without having such a close-knit family, the family business would not have been possible, and there would be no story to tell. Thank you for being who you are – caring, kind, considerate, and passionate about the success of the family business.

To my husband, Claude, the love of my life: Thank you for supporting me from day one. I can't imagine my life without you. You are my best friend. I love you!

I want to thank the agents that were ever a part of our team. I have learned from each of you, and I am grateful.

And to our Fontaine Team members, my extended family: You have been so helpful and so supportive throughout this project, and I thank you. I truly appreciate the value that each of you brings to our family team.

THE LIMITLESS REAL ESTATE LEADER

Building a Successful Business, Family, and Legacy

"Don't Let Anyone Steal Your Dream. It's Your Dream, not Theirs."

Dan Zandra

Nationally Recognized Author
Founder of Compendium, Inc.

INTRODUCTION

Writing a book on how to build a successful real estate career has been on my bucket list for many years. I just kept talking about it. "I'm going to write a book someday." The problem is "someday" never comes.

This past year I thought about it more often. Then I finally decided to take action and took the first step by calling a business coach I know. I knew that in order to get started, I needed accountability. Accountability works.

FULFILLING A PROMISE

I made a promise to God that if I were to become successful in the real estate business I would share my knowledge and success tips with others and help them become successful. I kept that promise early on by teaching everything I had learned; every single little secret I could share, I did.

This book is my continuation of fulfilling that promise that I made decades ago.

My goal is to inspire you to believe in yourself and to realize that if someone like me can build a successful real estate business, so can you!

Maybe you have fears, like I did. It's your choice not to let your fears control your life. You simply have to push through the fear

---

of failure and just do it. Your fears will never disappear. You must feel the fear and do it anyway.

So many people have inspired me over the years – those who meant to inspire me, and those who didn't.

Many great inspirational books by Tony Robbins, John Maxwell, Oprah, and Joel Osteen have been extremely valuable in my journey. I have also been inspired by several of the nation's top REALTORS®. They have been my self-appointed mentors.

Local REALTORS® who tried to discourage me actually inspired me. I had a lot of agents tell me that the team system would not work. "Clients only want to work with one agent. They don't want to work with a team. They want personalized service." Well, we were able to prove that clients love the team system because it offers the best personalized, world-class service you can get.

"Expanding to a second location is not a good idea! They don't know you, and they don't even know how to pronounce your name – Fontaine." Wow! That really hurt! But it also lit a fire inside me. I was determined to prove them all wrong – and I did! When people try to discourage you, you can't allow them to make your fears stronger. You must make your dream bigger instead and your will stronger. It makes for a sweeter victory!

When I was a single agent closing an average of 50 transactions a year, one of the agents in my company approached me after our awards banquet and commented on my success. Rather than congratulating me, she said, "Brenda, you have already reached your peak; you have nowhere to go now but down!" I just smiled and thought to myself, "Don't you wish; I will prove you wrong!"

Besides thanking all those who believed in me, like my mom and dad and my hubby, I really must thank those who tried to discourage me because they helped me tremendously to work even harder, and they made my burning desire stronger.

So don't be quick to shut off your dreams because of the critics. Don't let their opinions squash your goals. Just because they don't have the courage to push through their own fears, they don't want to see you succeed. Prove them wrong, and listen to your heart. If you're looking for a better life for you and your family, please know that anything is possible. You just need to get out of your comfort zone and do it – one small baby step at a time. Just go for it! Will it be easy? No! Will it be worth it? Yes!

"We Generate Fears While We Sit. We Overcome Them By Action."

Dr. Henry Link

Psychologist

CHAPTER 1

WHAT I LEARNED FROM MOM AND DAD

G rowing up with an alcoholic parent is a very difficult life and often quite frightening.

I grew up in a modest home on the outskirts of Lewiston, Maine. Our family home was built by my father and grandfather. My dad was so proud to tell me the story about how it took two full years to build it. Our house was built from the very trees that once stood on our ten-acre parcel of land. My grandfather had purchased 100 acres when land was dirt cheap and we were fortunate enough to have ten of those acres. It was a two-bedroom storybook cape with an unfinished second floor and a one-car garage under. Our kitchen cabinets and all our flooring were from scraps and surplus left at the city dump that my dad and I found from months of weekly treasure hunts. I really looked forward to those trips to the city dump. Dad was just as excited as I was, especially when we found something we could bring home.

Mom had no interest in joining us. She was either too sick, too tired, or too depressed. Seeing my mom in bed was the norm.

While Mom stayed home trying to cope with her fear of dying and her alcoholism, Dad worked 12-14 hour days, 6-7 days a week, owning and operating Ivan's Auto Body Shop.

Frankly, I often wondered if Dad worked so many hours just to get away from my mom's verbal, mental, and physical abuse or if he just loved his work. It was probably both.

I have a number of sad memories of this time in my life. One memory that haunts me is a 911 incident when I was 13.

I woke up from a sound sleep to high-pitched screams from my parents' bedroom. My mom was screaming at the top of her lungs, and my dad was shouting, "Stop it; please STOP!"

After jumping out of bed, I ran across the hallway to their bedroom door and immediately tried to turn the doorknob. The door was locked.

The screaming and shouting was nonstop – my heart was racing, and my mouth was dry from pure fear. Everything became a blur.

They were fighting again, except this time it was different. They were behind a locked door.

Typically my mom would be chasing my dad with a broom or a frying pan. Sometimes he would escape by running out the door. Once he got out the door and in the driveway, my mom would stop. I'm not sure if it was because it was too much trouble for her or maybe she didn't want the neighbor to be a witness to her abuse.

I decided to try to get their attention by screaming to let me in, but there was no reaction. Then I decided to grab a glass from the kitchen counter and throw it against the door hard, hoping the sound of broken glass would get them to snap out of it. But all I accomplished was creating a shower of tiny bits of pieces of glass everywhere and cutting myself in the process by stepping in it barefoot. Then there was blood all over the hallway. My efforts did not get their attention.

So I dialed 911 and through tears told the dispatcher that my mom and dad were fighting, and if someone didn't come soon, something very bad was going to happen.

After what felt like an eternity, two police cars drove up into our driveway.

I let them in and immediately showed them to the master bedroom. They asked me about the blood, and I told them what I had done and showed them the cuts on the soles of my feet.

When the police identified themselves, the screams immediately stopped, and the door was opened. One of the police officers asked me to go into the living room. They wanted to speak to my parents alone. I didn't see the inside of the bedroom. I was actually scared to look in.

A few minutes later, I heard the front door open and close. When I looked out the window, I saw my dad being taken out in handcuffs and placed in the back seat of the police car. I could feel a new stream of tears running down my cheeks and down my neck.

They had taken the wrong person. My dad would take the blame. Little did they know that Mom was the abuser in our family – not Dad. I should have had the courage to tell them.

I should have run out and shouted "No, you have the wrong person." But I was frozen in fear. I was scared to death of my mom. I knew she was mentally ill, even at that young age. I also knew she was capable of killing me or my dad. So I played it safe, and said nothing.

After the police car left, my mom came into the living room and said, "I know you wish I was the one they had taken. I know you love your father more than me."

My dad came back home that night, and no one ever talked about that day again.

Once I became a teenager, I wondered if I could get the courage to leave home and go and live on my own. I daydreamed a lot about finding my prince charming, getting married, having kids and a home of my own. I didn't expect my prince charming to support me – I wanted to find a job I would truly enjoy. I thought of nursing, but I knew that would require college, and I knew deep down there was no money for a college education. But that wouldn't deter me from my dreams.

I believe that the adversities experienced in my earlier years caused me to have that burning desire to succeed, and to live a better life than my parents.

I know my dad wanted a better life for himself and his family, and I know he did everything he could to make that happen. He had dreams. He wanted to own his own business.

After many years of hard work and scrimping and saving, he was able to become the owner of an auto body repair shop that also sold gas. I actually pumped gas there in my teenage years.

Dad worked long hours to make ends meet. He died at the age of 53 of stomach cancer. I was so proud of my dad and the fact that I was the daughter of Ivan Robert, the owner of Ivan's Auto Body Shop. He had worked on the family farm, holding on to the dream of becoming a business owner someday. He did realize his dream and left a legacy of strong work ethic, honesty, and integrity – and he will always be my hero. Whenever I mentioned my dad's name, I always heard positive comments saying what a good man he was.

Dad had come a long way, considering he only made it to fifth grade. It was not because he wasn't smart that he quit school. He quit to help out on the family's farm on Old Webster Road.

One of the most important lessons that I learned from my dad is that your reputation is one of the most important characteristics if you want to own your own business.

"It takes a long time to build a good reputation, but a bad one will spread like wildfire." – Ivan L. Robert

"Brenda, you must always tell the truth, go out of your way for your customers, and always do what's right."

I wondered if he thought I might someday take over his business. Little did I know at the time that those words would stay with me forever and guide me throughout my life.

My dad did not let his lack of education hold him back, and I wasn't going to let it hold me back either. We all have more potential than we can possibly imagine. I decided not to let my history determine my destiny – and you can do the same.

We must step out of our little safe world. We must stop limiting ourselves.

Don't wait for fear to disappear because it never will. Just push through it – and do it!

Don't let fear get between you and your dreams.

For years I had a terrible fear of flying. I missed out on so many incredible free trips that I had earned through my national franchise. I was honored multiple times as "Top All Around Agent" (one of the most prestigious national awards). Scotland was one of those trips that I declined because of my fear of flying.

Then I received the same award the following year; this time, it was a trip to Maui. I knew it was a long flight, but I decided to choose to push through the fear and go. The fear was still there. But I did it!

The flight was very smooth, but very long. It was an amazing and memorable trip. I'm very happy that my husband and I had such a great opportunity. I finally realized I could travel a long distance and survive. Each trip became easier. I never expected to ever travel to California. And now my husband and I have been there numerous times. I never expected to travel to Europe. Last year we flew to Amsterdam and took an eight-day Viking cruise to ports in Holland, France, Germany, and Switzerland.

If I had allowed my fear to stay in control of my life, I would still be paralyzed in that "small, safe world." And I would never have gotten into real estate.

I also learned some valuable business lessons from my mom. She eventually joined AA after many trips to detox centers. She did stop drinking for years at a time, and life was good during those years.

Mom became an Avon Lady during those sober years, and that was the beginning of my sales career. She would drive me to the territory that was assigned to her. She then would hand me a basket of Avon products, along with dozens of Avon brochures, and tell me to go door knocking and ask the lady of the house if she would be interested. She trained me on what to say and how to fill out the order forms. I was extremely successful, and I actually loved it.

Most of the ladies could not say "no" to a young, 14-year-old girl who looked like 12.

The money earned went to my mom. But my mom gave me a lot of free products.

We also started booking Beeline Fashion parties. I modeled the clothes, and I got all my school clothes free.

By the time I was 16, I was prospecting on the phone and booking fashion show home parties until we switched over to Fashion Two Twenty cosmetics. I continued to book parties, now for Fashion Two Twenty, and started recruiting other sales reps. Little did I know at that time, but my mom laid the foundation for a successful sales career for me decades later.

While I drew many positive traits from my parents, I also had positive influences from unexpected family members.

I met the love of my life three months after graduating from high school and after the breakup of a serious 3-1/2 year relationship.

I met my husband Claude when he picked me up at the home of a boy I was dating. Yes, that's the short version. My friend's boyfriend's car had broken down, and Claude stopped to help them out – and that choice he made to help a friend that night led him to meet me.

Within three months he asked me to marry him. We only dated ten months before marrying. And 9-1/2 months later, our twin daughters were born – two years to the day of my high school graduation.

Claude worked for my dad at the body shop after quitting hand sewing at the shoe shop. Claude had quit school as a sophomore because he did not speak a word of English. He was French Canadian and his parents moved to the US when Claude was 14. I met him when he was 20. He never graduated from high school.

Claude worked long hours for my dad, and I stayed home taking care of the twins. They were my world! We lived from paycheck to paycheck. Many times there wasn't even a paycheck, but we found a way to make it work.

I kept trying to find work. Then one day I finally received a call from Liberty Mutual. I had done very well on a math test, and they had an opening for me in their Workmen's Comp department.

I enjoyed that job, and I loved the people I worked with. But after about four years, I was totally bored. I found myself watching the clock all day, wishing my life away. I needed something more challenging. I also longed for the day I could be home for the twins when they would come home from school. I decided to get back in direct sales to supplement our income. So I chose Fashion Two Twenty cosmetics, and I once again did very well. Then I accidentally got pregnant with our third daughter. Once she was born, that would be the end of my home parties with Fashion Two Twenty.

I knew she would be our last baby, and I wanted to enjoy every moment.

I also knew that there was no way I could find a job and pay daycare for three little girls. So I decided to start my own daycare once my baby turned one. I put my heart and soul in my licensed, daycare business. I loved the kids. I had all ages from infancy to school age. I loved teaching preschool to the 3-, 4-, and 5-year-olds.

But after about three years, the everyday stress of having ten kids from 6AM to 6PM started to take its toll on my health. And again, I knew it was time for a change. By then the twins, Missy and Angie, were nearly ten, and Crystal was nearly four.

I had lots of medical tests because of headaches and stomach problems. They found nothing. The doctor told me it was stress. I started toying with the idea of taking courses to become a paralegal. Unfortunately, my professional aspirations were once again sidetracked.

One Sunday afternoon (while I was taking a nap at the same time as Crystal, now 3-1/2 years old) Claude woke me up to tell me the twins had fallen out of his moving pickup truck. We needed to get them to the hospital fast.

We took Crystal to our friend and neighbor, and rushed our nine-year-old twins to St. Mary's General Hospital in Lewiston. They were both very sleepy. I didn't know much about concussions or brain injuries, but I did know that I needed to keep them awake.

So I kept talking to them all the way to the hospital, telling them to stay awake and not to fall asleep even though they were very sleepy. It was a long three-mile ride, but I was able to keep them awake by just talking to them non-stop.

The medical staff took them right away, and that's when I heard the whole story. Claude was taking truckloads of wood from the wood lot down the road to our house (back and forth). The girls had been in the back of the pickup. On this particular load, Claude did not notice the girls had moved to the tailgate and were sitting on the very edge. When Claude hit a bump in the road, the tailgate let go and the girls were dumped, hitting their heads on the paved surface.

When Claude heard the noise of the tailgate dropping, he looked in his rearview mirror and saw his two little girls lying in the middle of the road like rag dolls.

Thank God that Old Webster Road was a very quiet country road back then because they could have been run over.

I will never forget the look on his face when he told me. I never had seen so much terror in his eyes as I did that afternoon.

The twins did stay in the hospital for several days. They both had suffered concussions and skull fractures. Claude stayed by their side nights. I had taken time off from daycare and stayed with them during the day while someone babysat Crystal. Thanks to God, the twins made a full recovery. Our prayers were answered.

My continuing education was put on hold. I felt this was a sign that I had to put my family first.

I couldn't bear the thought of leaving them and getting a full-time job outside the home. We had almost lost our twin girls. I decided I wasn't ready for any kind of change yet.

So it would be another year before quitting daycare came back into my thoughts, and it was my husband who started the conversation.

It was the summer of 1982. We were driving to our friends' house, when my husband Claude brought up the idea that I should get into real estate. He knew that the wife of an auto body man had done quite well and had seen her picture in the paper. The ad read that she was a million dollar producer. And my husband told me, "If she can do it, you can do it too."

I had been enjoying the beautiful countryside of Minot, but after he mentioned his idea, I started squirming in my seat. I felt agitated. I replied, "Claude, you can't count on real estate. It's too risky. We need a steady income, a weekly paycheck. We can't afford it."

I had been a licensed daycare provider for four years, and I knew I was ready for a change. My husband knew it too. I had continued to suffer from stomach problems and headaches. We dropped the subject that day, but he had planted the seed.

Then a few months later, I saw an ad in the paper that read:

"Dream Job
Flexible Hours
Unlimited Income Potential
A Career in Real Estate"

The ad motivated me to make that call and go for an interview. I asked a lot of questions. I was interested in finding out how I was going to get business.

The office manager told me I would be responsible to get my own business. She said I would need to call "For Sale by Owners" and sellers whose listing contracts had expired.

When I asked about answering the phones to get buyers, she said I needed to get my own business first. She gave me all the information I needed to take the real estate classes in order to prepare for the state exam.

I decided to go for it!

I thought I would start part-time and still keep the daycare going. I would study while my daycare kids were napping. I would study on weekends. I was determined to pass the state exam. Unfortunately, I did not pass the first time – I missed it by one point. I didn't give up; I went back and took it again.

I'll always remember the day I walked over to the mailbox and pulled out the envelope from the state. I tore open the envelope and saw my passing grade. I literally jumped with joy, looked up at the sky, and said, "Thank you, Jesus!"

I truly felt that a whole new world was opening up for me and my family.

I was so proud to let everyone know that I was a REALTOR®. My part-time idea lasted all of two weeks.

I was enjoying the work so much I knew I had to do it full-time. I gave my daycare parents a two-week notice and then decided to take the risk of going full time. I knew I had found my passion.

I remember seeing my sister-in-law at my husband's auto body shop my first year in the business. We were standing in the parking lot by our vehicles, and she asked me how I was doing in the real estate business. I said, "This job is just too good to be true. I am so worried that something bad is going to happen because I'm just too happy."

I guess I had had so many bad things happen in my life that I just could not believe that good things could happen too.

If only those who had made fun of me in grade school could see me now – those bullies who made fun of my soiled clothes. They didn't know my mom was too sick to do laundry and my dad was too busy working.

Those years growing up, I had a dream that someday I would be really good at something. I actually wanted to be better than good. I wanted to excel at something. I wanted to be the best of the best at something. I had finally found that "something" and that "something" was Real Estate.

FIVE LESSONS FROM MY EARLY YEARS

1. Do not let fear prevent you from reaching your goals.

2. Your reputation is your best business card.

3. If you take care of your customers, they will pay you back in many ways.

4. Your limitations are only the ones you place on yourself.

5. You can learn positive lessons from negative situations.

"Success Is Nothing More than a Few Simple Disciplines, Practiced Every Day."

Jim Rohn

National Speaker and Award Winner

CHAPTER 2

GETTING STARTED

E ven though I was excited about becoming a REALTOR®, I knew that I had a lot to learn. The first important task was identifying the agency with which I wanted to work. I had a number of important characteristics in my mind to determine where I would hang my shingle.

After I had interviewed with the first real estate agency, I gathered all the info I needed to study and prepare for the exam. I decided to visit the other four real estate companies in our community.

I would recommend you do the same, if you're at the beginning stages. You need to be sure you choose the right fit for you.

My decision was definitely based on being the right fit. But I also paid close attention to whose For Sale signs I saw the most in the front yards of my community. Of course, the broker/owner, the culture, and the training available were huge factors as well. Also, since I had zero money to invest, joining a company that would pay for most of the expenses was very important.

So I decided on ERA.

For the four months I was studying and preparing for the state exam, I was also preparing my prospecting list. When I was exhausted with studying, I was compiling my list of family and friends. I had been told by one of the broker/owners that 250 was a good number for a sphere of influence list. I was also clipping newspaper ads of "For Sale by Owners" and house rentals every day. I was doing this while my daycare kids were napping.

When I had asked the broker where I would get my leads, I was told, "People you know, For Sale by Owners, houses for rent, and expired listings" (homes that were listed but failed to sell during their contract period).

I was preparing so that as soon as I was licensed, I would immediately be ready to pick up the phone and start prospecting. That preparation proved to be very profitable.

If you haven't made your 250 list yet, do it now – even if you don't have your license yet. Just get it done. By being prepared, you'll be ahead of everyone else that's in your sales agent class.

If you are experienced, and it's been a while since you sent your sphere anything, do it. Send them an item of value. It could be valuable real estate info that could help them save money or help them get more money for their home when they get ready to sell. They will appreciate your help, and when they are ready to sell, they'll remember you helped them.

Because I was prepared, I was ready to start prospecting on my first day becoming a licensed sales associate. And I did!

I had four months' worth of newspaper clippings of For Sale by Owner, and I dived right into lead generating. What I didn't realize at the time was that having this list of homeowners who had been trying to sell for two, three, and four months was a golden opportunity. You see, they were ready for a REALTOR®

to help them. It wasn't that I was that good or that skilled at speaking to For Sale by Owner prospects. They were ready to hear how I could help.

Did I get some rejections? Of course. Rejection was not going to discourage me. Once I had made the decision to be a real estate agent, I was committed to doing the work that needed to be done to earn a paycheck. I had never been afraid of hard work. Besides my direct sales experience helping my mom, I had also worked at my dad's body shop pumping gas, and preparing cars for spray painting by scuffing and taping the chrome, bumpers, and windows. We would use old newspapers and masking tape. I also did this until I was eight months pregnant with the twins.

I was so excited to have passed that state exam! I graduated from high school and had taken college courses throughout my high school years, but I was far from being an "A" student. I was an average student.

To me, a real estate career meant a step up in the world. I believed I had entered the world of business professionals at the highest level. I was so proud of my new career.

I wanted to climb on the highest rooftops and shout, "I'm a REALTOR®!"

Back then I didn't realize that real estate agents were not as respected as they are today. I know that there are great agents that are professional and have strong work ethics and strong values. They care about their reputations. They do right by their clients. And they really care and always look out for their best interest. And these agents are the ones that last and that are successful.

When your clients know that your word is good, and that you will always be truthful even if it's not what they want to hear, they will respect you for it. When you're focused on their goals, they will never forget. They will tell their family and friends that you helped them get through a stressful time.

As I said earlier, when I first started, I was still operating my daycare and doing real estate on a part-time basis. I was operating my daycare 12 hours a day, 5 days a week, 6 AM to 6 PM, and doing real estate nights and weekends. My number one goal was to prospect For Sale by Owners. So I would call and ask to see the house to determine if I could help to get it sold.

I truly believed I could help. I believed it with my whole heart, and I spoke with conviction and enthusiasm. I prepared and practiced my listing presentation at my kitchen table. I did my presentation to an empty chair every night I didn't have a listing appointment. I believe continuous improvement and continuous learning are necessary for getting positive results.

Whenever I sent a mail-out, my daughters helped by stuffing the envelopes. It was a family affair even back then.

There comes a time when you have to go out there and do it. You learn more by actually being involved in the process.

As soon as I was licensed, one of my daycare parents decided to sell their mobile home. My broker arranged to have an experienced agent come with me for support and guidance, but she had to cancel at the last minute.

But the Lebels made it easy for me. They just asked me where to sign and the mobile home went under contract within a couple of weeks. Then they became buyers. I showed them several homes, and they bought a ranch with a two-car garage on a couple of acres. They are still clients today, and they have bought and sold with us numerous times over three decades.

The following week my cousin called and told me he wanted to buy a multi-unit. I showed him several buildings and within a week, he put a four-unit under contract. This would be my very first closing. And it was exactly six weeks from the day my license was issued.

Meanwhile, I was booking listing appointments like I had booked home parties. And within a few weeks, I had a handful of listings.

Even though I was very nervous, I pushed through the fear, and I did it anyway.

My first For Sale by Owner was a memorable experience. The homeowner was a widow in her late fifties. I asked her if she could take me through the house first, and then we could sit and talk. I also asked her if I could place my material on her kitchen table. She agreed.

As we toured her meticulous home, she pointed to photos on her wall of her husband and family. She shared her precious memories with me. I listened and asked questions and enjoyed her heartwarming stories.

After we went back to the kitchen table to sit, I asked her where she was moving and when she was hoping to make the move. She was moving in with her daughter, and she hoped to be settled before the first snowfall.

As I was going through my presentation, she listened attentively. She was asking $45,000 (this was 1983). After reviewing the comparable sales, I recommended $49,900.

I filled out a net sheet so she would see what her bottom line would be after paying her closing costs. She was in agreement with the bottom line, so I asked if she was ready to allow me to help her get the house sold, and she said, "Yes!"

I walked out of that house with such a high. I felt I could conquer the world. This was a complete stranger, and she trusted me to sell her home. I was honored. I wasn't going to let her down. And it did go under contract within the week.

I had three properties under contract my first two weeks working part-time.

After two weeks I asked my broker/owner if he thought I could make $2,000 a month.

My daycare business was contributing $24,000 a year to our household income, and we really needed that income. He convinced me that I could make that and more.

So I took the leap and gave my daycare parents a two-week notice. I would be closing my daycare operation by mid-October. It had only taken me two weeks to make the decision to go full-time in real estate. It was a big risk. Because it was a big risk, failure was not an option. My daycare business helped pay the bills and buy groceries. It wasn't for extras or vacations.

I treated my new real estate career as a real job. Most agents don't. That's why 95% of the business is done by 5% of the agents. You must go into the office at the same time each day unless you have an appointment. Start as early as you can. Showing up is the first step to treating it like a real job.

I prospected four nights a week for 2-3 hours. If I had secured two listing appointments, I would allow myself to end my prospecting early. If not, I would continue three hours straight. Many nights I would get my two appointments within a two-hour period. Once in a while, I would get them within an hour.

I didn't have a complicated business plan. It was quite simple. I knew that in real estate, in order to have buyers, you needed inventory. Inventory is listings. If you have listings, you attract buyers.

My goal was to go on 2-4 listing appointments a week. I didn't always reach my goal, but I always managed to get 3-4 listings a month. I was able to reach that goal because I was consistent in my prospecting activity. And I was very good at following up at the exact day and time the owner gave me permission to do so. I just booked it in my schedule as an appointment. And I followed up religiously.

I would become very nervous the rare times when I had no listing appointments. But it just motivated me to make the calls, because I felt unemployed when I had no appointments ahead of me. I felt very accomplished when I was filling up my calendar with listing appointments and showings. The more inventory I had, the more buyers I was getting. The phone started ringing off the hook.

I continued to read everything I could about how to be the best real estate agent I could be. I didn't want to be your average agent; I wanted to be extraordinary.

I found out quickly that listening to your sellers and buyers and being able to feel their pain would help me advise them. It was not always in the family's best interest to sell their home because of the situation they were in. If they owed more than their house was worth, and they were not in a financial hardship (in other words, they could still afford their mortgage payment), I would advise them not to sell. I would tell them it was better to wait until the market appreciated. When you do what's right and treat your clients like family, they will be loyal to you. It is not about you or me; it's about putting your clients first and putting their interest first – not yours. It's also about creating client relationships for life by making your clients feel important. Many of our Fontaine clients repeatedly say they felt like they were our only clients. That's how you must always make your clients feel.

"Build your business by building a database of client relationships, not a database of just names." – Brian Buffini

When I was searching for a milestone that first year, I asked my husband Claude what stood out to him in my first year in the business. He said, "We were finally able to buy a riding lawn mower." That was our first major purchase since we had bought our home seven years earlier through the FHA 235 program. Through that program we were able to get a 5% interest rate that was adjustable based on income. It did increase to 8% after my first full year in real estate.

My husband was thrilled the day we brought the John Deere home in the spring of 1984. He had been pushing a lawn mower on a three-acre lawn for nearly 13 years. We moved into our mobile home right after our honeymoon in September 1971. We moved into our newly built home in November of 1976.

I had a number of memorable experiences my very first year in the business, and I will share the best one and the worst one with you.

One of my first listing appointments was another For Sale by Owner. The home was on the market for $89,900. That was considered high end back in 1983; the average sale price was $35,000. The gentleman was very cordial. He shook my hand and welcomed me. He had a beautiful 2,500 square foot home in a great neighborhood. It was the most beautiful home I had ever been in. I was so nervous that I was shaking like a scared puppy. But he didn't seem to notice. I began by asking him questions, trying to keep the focus off me. He was getting transferred and needed to sell yesterday. It didn't take him long to start asking me questions. He wanted to know what I thought of the salability of the home and what I thought it was worth, because he wanted to know if he was at the right price. I shared my sales data with him. I was very well prepared, and I shared how I could help get his home sold.

He told me he was interviewing two other agents. I did gather up the courage to ask him who the other agents were. He wouldn't tell me, but I knew whoever they were, they more than likely had more experience than I did. I was determined to follow up, so I asked when he would be meeting with the two agents. Then I asked his permission to follow up with a phone call. And he said, "Yes."

When I followed up the next week, he told me he had decided on ME! I was so excited to have beaten out two other agents, but I had to know why he chose me. And he said, "It's your enthusiasm!"

Wow! My enthusiasm! It wasn't my presentation, it wasn't my ERA franchise or my company's reputation, and it wasn't my opinion of value. It was my enthusiasm. The home did go under contract within a few weeks, and he wrote a beautiful letter of recommendation after the closing.

So for the "newbies" out there, don't let fear paralyze you because you don't have experience. You need to prepare, study the market, know the inventory, and just do it. Start going on appointments. You will learn more by doing. Of course, you should job shadow for a few weeks. You also should have a mentor your first six months. Ask to shadow a successful agent.

My least successful experience that first year was the day I showed a home with 17 acres on the outskirts of Auburn. It was in the spring, so I had been in real estate for about seven months. I still believed real estate was a glamorous career. I made a daily effort to look professional. On this particular day, I wore a fitted red dress with a high scoop neck, and the length was just above my knees (not too short). I chose a pair of high-heeled, black sandals to match my thin black belt.

The couple chose to meet me at the house. We toured the house first, and they loved it. They wanted me to show them the land next. So I thought I would clarify and said, "So you want to walk the land?" and they said, "Yes."

Being the trooper that I am and excited about the fact that they loved the house, I enthusiastically responded, "Sure, follow me!"

I had no idea what was in store for any of us. What started off as an easy walking nature trail turned into a hike up a steep hill and down a muddy valley. I sunk in mud to my ankles repeatedly, but I kept going, hoping they wouldn't notice.

At one point, the hem of my dress somehow got caught on a small branch, causing my dress to be hiked up to my waist and exposing my behind. Back then, I wore Underalls (which were a type of pantyhose that didn't require underwear). I turned sideways as best I could, but I couldn't turn enough to be able to free myself. Then I saw male hands reaching out to help me. I was too embarrassed to make eye contact. So I just said "Thank you," and without giving it any thought I blurted out in frustration, "Have you guys seen enough?"

Unamused, the wife quickly said, "Yes, we sure have!" There was complete silence back to the house. I couldn't get to my car fast enough.

They said they'd call me, and I prayed they wouldn't.

When I looked down at my feet, I could not see my sandals. Anyone would think that I was wearing boots that were covered in mud. It was that bad.

From that day forward I would be better prepared to walk land.

By the way, my prayers were answered. They never did call. Even though my first year was full of many more positive signs than negative, I knew in my heart that some adjustments were necessary as I moved forward.

FIVE LESSONS FROM MY FIRST YEAR IN BUSINESS

1. Prospecting consistently and following up religiously brings positive results.

2. Your enthusiasm can help you overcome your inexperience or shaky confidence.

3. If you're going to go for it, give it your all.

4. This is a business, not a hobby.

5. Dress appropriately (LOL).

"Talent Wins Games, but Teamwork and Intelligence Wins Championships."

Michael Jordan

Retired Professional Basketball Player

CHAPTER 3

THE FAMILY BUSINESS

My first year was very successful, but very challenging. I decided I needed to make a change of affiliation. I wasn't getting the support that I needed and I wasn't happy with the culture. It felt like I was back in school. I would be called out for being a few minutes late to the meeting or I would be called to the "principal's" office because I had not parked my car exactly between the lines. There was no mentoring or sharing of ideas. I had asked one of the agents for help, and I was told that she didn't share any of her secrets because we were all in competition with each other. Even though I was just a rookie, I didn't know much, but what I did know was that this was not the environment I wanted to work in. I knew it was not a good fit for me. I moved across the river in Auburn to another ERA franchise. And I would be there for the next 25 years.

I had 19 properties under contract when I left. So I had to return to my "ex" agency many times to pick up the files and go to the closings and return with the file and closing check in order to get paid. It was very awkward and uncomfortable, but I got through it.

I had told a couple of agents I wasn't happy and that I was thinking of leaving and joining the other ERA agency. I had actually planned on leaving two weeks later, but word got out; I was summoned to the manager's office, asked for the office key, and told to clean out my desk and leave immediately. So I did.

I had a closing to attend that day, and I was concerned I would be late if I had to clean my desk right away. But I was not given a choice.

So I rushed and threw everything in a box and left. No time for "goodbyes" either.

I did make it on time to my closing, and returned the file to the manager immediately after the closing.

When I got home that night, I had a good cry. I started questioning whether or not I could be as successful at my new agency. Was it just luck? Did I really have what it takes to have continued success?

I cried every night straight for a good week and a half. I would lie in bed at night unable to sleep, questioning my decision, and fearing for the worst. During the day, I walked around with a wicked headache, but always put a smile on my face and moved on. I look back on it today and realize how much worrying was a waste of time.

Do you worry needlessly? Do you fear the unknown? Do you realize that most everything we worry about never happens? I wish I had realized that years ago. We can never get back all that time. I always tried to learn from other people's mistakes. Hope you can learn from mine.

Even though I worried, I kept going. I put one foot in front of the other and took it one step at a time. I kept going into the office every day. Everyone was extremely friendly. It was like a family. I kept up my daily habit of prospecting.

My business continued to grow, and I continued to learn from the people around me, especially my new broker/owner Tim. I truly believe my thirst for knowledge played a major role in my success. Don't ever stop learning. It's the best investment you'll ever make. That and not being afraid of taking educated risks.

In 1995 ERA had a six-week training program called Top Gun. I had been in the business for 12 years, but I was always looking for ways to improve (and I still do today). Top Gun was similar to Floyd Wickman, a national real estate training program. It was all about prospecting, accountability, and staying focused and motivated. Everyone needs accountability and motivation, even agents who have been top in their field. Even if I just got one new thing, it would be worth it.

That one thing happened on the day that the instructor, Dustin, asked everyone to write their goals on a piece of paper.

Well, my goal since the first year in the business had been 50 closings a year. (The national average for agent closings is seven closed units annually.) And I was proud and content to reach that goal year after year. My broker would always compliment me on how consistent I was.

So I wrote "50" on my notepad. Then, after a few seconds of silence, the instructor said, "OK, now that you have jotted down a number, I want you to double it."

What? Double it? "Write your new goal!" I had never heard anyone say, "Double your goal." I felt I had a big enough goal. I thought to myself, "Is he crazy? I already have a big goal." But I still wrote the number "100." I decided to play along. After all, this was private. But I did feel uncomfortable with that number. Then he said, "Now write down what you need to do differently to reach that goal."

I wrote, "Hire a full-time assistant."

Up until then, I had only hired very part-time help. Another agent and I had finally taken a baby step in hiring a part-time assistant for eight hours a week. We each paid for four hours. It wasn't much, but it was something.

It's better to take baby steps than taking no steps at all.

After a few months, I could have had her work more hours, but she was an older lady and she had no desire to work more. By that point my daughter Melissa was coming in occasionally to do mail-outs for me.

What would this full-time licensed assistant do? Definitely answer the phone, do paperwork, set up showings, etc. And that would free me up to actually work more with clients.

Hmm... My wheels were spinning, and I could see how it could work. And I have always had big dreams. One of my dreams was to buy a motor home and take lots of road trips to all the places we had never been, and that was just about everywhere except New England and Canada. We had traveled to Disney World by van with the family several times. Motor home traveling would be a dream come true. Back then I had a fear of flying, so we were very limited on where to travel.

So I wrote, "Buy a motor home and travel to Florida and other states with the family making memories." That would be my "Why?" What about you? What do you think could happen if you doubled your goal? I truly believe that if you put a plan in place to double your goal, you would reach it.

But you also need a "Why" – Why double your goal? What is your dream? Is it a down payment on a home? Is it a vacation home on the water? Maybe it's a new car. Maybe it's your kids' college education. What is your "Why"? Write it down. Now go for it! You can do it. Never give up. It will happen! Believe in yourself – and the sky is the limit.

So as soon as I returned, I immediately went on the hunt to find a licensed assistant. There was a new agent in our agency who was struggling, and the word around the office was that she was thinking of quitting. Kelly had been with us just a few months.

I approached her and asked if she would be interested in working for me 30 hours a week. I told her she would be working alongside of me, answering calls, doing listing paperwork, and setting up showings. She gladly accepted the position. It was perfect for her, and it was perfect for me.

That first full year Kelly was with me, we did reach our goal. Actually we exceeded it a little. We closed 102 properties. I went from 50 closings a year to 102 by having one licensed assistant work 30 hours a week. She more than paid for herself.

And by the way, we did purchase that motor home and traveled to Disney with the family. We continued to make many wonderful memories traveling to different areas and camping. The fact that I took action as soon as I returned, while everything was fresh and I was still excited, made it easier for me to reach my goal.

Whenever I take a class or a seminar, I always make an effort to implement something when I return home. It's impossible to implement everything, but focus on at least one thing and then take the action necessary. Without action, nothing happens.

What is the one thing that you have heard lately that could impact your business? Whatever that is, don't wait any longer. Start implementing today. Take action today! What can you do right now to start the wheel in motion?

"Education without implementation is merely entertainment."
– Brian Buffini

I had no idea at the time how this one thing – this one statement that Dustin Secor, the instructor, had suggested – would have such a huge impact on the direction of my future.

And even though Melissa was coming in now and then to do mail-outs for me, the idea of having a family business never entered my mind. Then something unexpected happened. Melissa was laid off temporarily from Geiger Bros.; she wanted to know if I had any work for her to do until she was called back. And I actually did. I had her research names and phone numbers of "For Sale by Owners" and "Expireds." She was working about 10-15 hours a week. I was always calling property owners to see if they wanted to sell and constantly trying to match them up with my current buyers. Once I exhausted my buyers, I would go around the office and ask my co-workers who they had for buyers, and ask them to describe what their buyers were looking for so I could match their buyers with my listings. It's amazing how many sales you can make when you're proactive and take control of your situation and work on making things happen. I loved matchmaking buyers and sellers. (And my agents have continued on with that tradition of being proactive and matching up buyers and sellers instead of waiting for them to call us. We call them.)

Well anyway, one day out of the blue, Kelly gave me her two-week notice due to family issues. I understood her dilemma because I'm a strong believer of family first. Now I was frantic to find a replacement. Kelly had been doing a good job, and I couldn't imagine what it would be like without her. So I started going around the office asking agents who were not busy if they had any interest. No one did.

Then my daughter Melissa, who was overhearing my conversations, piped up and said, "Mom, how about me?" My first reaction was, "No way!"

Melissa had been working for me on a very part-time basis on and off since she was 21. But she was doing mail-outs and running errands, and she did not have any direct contact with the clients. Besides, Melissa didn't have her real estate license, and she was extremely shy. I said, "I don't think so, Missy. You know you would have to talk to clients."

Missy said, "I know, Mom. I hear Kelly talk to clients, and I know I can do it. Just give me a chance."

I told her, "I would have to give it some thought."

Before I hired Kelly, I was constantly feeling overwhelmed. It was very difficult keeping everything straight. I was starting to feel guilty that I was shortchanging my clients. I was having a hard time keeping up with communicating the feedback after showings, as an example.

It's very important to know the feedback after every showing, not only to communicate that feedback to the seller, but also to analyze the feedback as a professional to figure out what we can do to motivate a buyer to write an offer. Most agents can't keep up with this important task because the days are already full for them.

If this is something you as an agent can't keep up with, and you can't respond to your clients within a few hours, it's time for you to get help.

Is it difficult to let go? Of course. But once you realize that others can do as good as you, and some can actually do better than you, you're on your way to giving the world-class service that every homeseller and homebuyer deserves.

So that night I visualized Melissa speaking to my clients. I knew Melissa was very patient. Claude and I had raised our daughters to be polite, kind, and considerate to others. So when I spoke to my husband about it, we both agreed that Melissa would be very good to the clients. I knew she had the patience, and I knew she was trustworthy.

So what was I worried about? I still saw her as my little girl even though she was a young adult. That was the problem. And I thought her shyness could be a handicap. Plus she was not licensed.

So the next day, I asked Melissa if she would be willing to take the real estate classes necessary to take the state exam to be licensed.

She agreed. I also told her that she needed to always refer to me as "Brenda" to clients and agents, and not "My mom." Example: "My mom's not here right now. Is there something I can help you with?" I wanted professionalism.

I also stopped calling her "Missy" at the office. Her real name is Melissa. Because of her age, and because I felt it would be professional, I asked her to refer to herself as "Melissa."

And so our first team family member was paving the way for more to come. Yet, no one had any idea. Not even me!

I am grateful that God gave me the vision to see how it could work and the courage to take the risk.

Trusting your instincts and giving others the opportunity to prove themselves can be a win-win.

Even though Melissa was helping me, she was also helping herself by being willing to get out of her comfort zone, like she had seen me do during her growing-up years.

You always wonder if what you are saying to your children really sticks with them. This was proof to me that Melissa had been listening.

Hiring a family member can be risky, but it can also be the best decision you could ever make. Only you can make that decision. It should be decided on a case-by-case basis. You must have the type of relationship where you can agree to disagree. You need to be open to new ideas, not just from family members but from everyone on your team. You also need to be open to criticism and not take any of it personally. It's not personal if it's business. It's easier said than done. But with practice, it gets easier.

I did find myself being so much harder on her than I had been with Kelly. Kelly was great, but I realized after she left that I had expected less from her. And yet, from the beginning I expected so much more from Melissa.

Kelly took messages for me; I always had tons of messages to return daily, and I accepted it. That's just the way it was.

With Melissa, I told her that I felt she should try to solve the problem right away. It would elevate our customer service, and she would be bringing more value to her position.

I still remember what I said to her about taking messages – something I should have told Kelly, but never had the nerve. But with family, there is no filter. So I said, "Missy, I don't need a message taker; I need a problem solver." And Melissa came through for me.

One thing I have realized over the years is that our kids are smarter and better people than we are in so many ways.

We need to always be open to their ideas and their suggestions. We should always be open to the ideas of those we trust. And then, make the final decision.

This was over 20 years ago, and I have never regretted the decision to hire Melissa or any family member, for that matter.

Today Melissa is our office manager, short sale specialist, and closing coordinator. She is very respected by all.

Hiring a family member can be risky, but it can also be the best decision you ever made. Working with your spouse, on the other hand, presents a whole other set of challenges.

Claude had been helping me behind the scenes, running personal as well as business errands, besides being an equal partner in an auto body shop business. He picked up our clothes at the dry cleaners, took the girls wherever they needed to go, and he would pick up keys for me, or put up a sign now and then. Whenever I was running out of time, he would come to my rescue. He always supported me in my business by giving me a helping hand whenever I asked.

The auto body work business has lots of "ups" and "downs." When business was slow, the owners would pay the bills and their employees, and then they would pay themselves if there was any money left. More often than not, there was no money left for either owner to get paid.

Claude could work all week for weeks at a time and bring home zero money. It was very discouraging for him and for me. This didn't just go on for weeks. It went on for years, on and off.

So one day I said to him, "Why don't you just come help me on a full-time basis? You're not making any money anyway. What do you have to lose?" I knew I could really use his help.

For a man to work so hard day after day and not bring home a paycheck for weeks at a time is not good for his self-esteem. He was unhappy. I knew it. Everyone knew it. So he took me up on the offer, but there would be challenges. My husband Claude had not graduated from high school because there was too much of a language barrier when he moved to the United States with his family. He was 14 and spoke no English whatsoever, nor could he understand one single word. His family had always lived at his paternal grandmother's house. His parents never owned their own home, so they traveled across the border in search of a better life. His dad was in search of a job that would offer him plenty of work in order to keep his family fed and to have a roof over their heads. The French Canadians never prayed or hoped for plenty of money. They prayed for plenty of work so they could keep their family fed and clothed. I'm so proud of my heritage, and so proud of my ancestors' strong work ethic. (Both my paternal and maternal grandparents were Canadian immigrants.)

Imagine Claude, as a young teen boy, who had to leave all his friends to move to a strange country. He had never seen the ocean. He had never been outside of the Province of Quebec. He was totally against the move, but it was not his decision.

Imagine walking into a high school in a foreign country, and not being able to speak or understand the language. He was transferred from school to different school, until they finally demoted him to 8th grade at a Catholic elementary school. He went on to Lewiston High School but quickly transferred to St. Dom's. There were more French-speaking students there who tried helping him. And he was very grateful, but it was still a challenge that he could not overcome.

He quit school as a sophomore and went to work full-time in the neighborhood bakery at 16 years old. His next job was as a hand sewer in a shoe shop, where he worked for the next few years. He did join the National Guard at 18, and he would be in the National Guard for seven years.

Two years later, he was working with my dad at the body shop. He would be in that line of work for nearly 20 years.

Claude had been working with me just running errands for a few months when I brought up the idea that he should get his GED so he could become a licensed real estate agent too.

I remember exactly where I was when I made the call. I was driving down Scribner Boulevard in Lewiston. I just picked up the cell phone and called him and said, "Claude, I've been thinking about you getting licensed, but you need to get your GED first. You know you're smart; I'm sure you would have no problem getting it."

At first he said, "No way!" He thought it would take too long. He pictured himself going to school for three years. He was dragging his feet, procrastinating and really had no interest at that time. So I made the initial call and gathered all the needed information for him. I kept encouraging him and told him he could do it. He finally took the initiative and within a few months he had his GED, and then qualified to take his real estate classes.

Melissa and Claude went to the real estate classes together and became officially licensed at the same time after successfully passing their state exam on the same day.

What I didn't realize at the time, though, was how challenging it would be to have my husband work with me. You see, Claude had been self-employed. He also had always been "the man of the house." I was 18 when we met and 19 when we were married. HE was the breadwinner. HE was the boss. Now, the roles were changing, and neither one of us realized how difficult it would be to adjust.

I will never forget the first day he came in full-time. He wanted to rearrange the furniture in my office, which would mean moving my desk. That was the first of many disagreements.

I said, "No, my desk is staying right where it is." I had to make him realize that just because he was joining me in the business didn't mean he was in charge. I was in charge of the real estate business. He was in charge at home.

We had disagreements on a daily basis. He would hear my conversations with clients and give me his advice on how I should have handled it. I would tell him, "This is not going to work; you need to go home." He would say, "I quit anyway."

I would give him advice on counseling his buyers, and he would reject my advice at first; but eventually he came around, and he listened.

I believe what helped us through this major change in our lives was that we never had any trouble communicating our issues to each other. So throughout our marriage, we had many arguments. We always said what was on our minds. We had no filters, but we never stayed upset with each other for very long. Neither one of us used "the silent treatment."

Over the years, we had several friend couples who never ever fought, and we were shocked when they divorced, but they never communicated. They never told each other how they felt about anything.

So we argued, and we said what we had to say, and then we would get over it. And everything would be back to normal. If he would interrupt me during a business call, I would lose my cool with him and get snippy. Once I cooled off, I would apologize, and we would both move on. But I would ask him not to interrupt me when I was busy with a client. Things did improve over time.

We began getting used to working together. Then he got busy showing houses, and putting up signs, and I was busy listing property and negotiating contracts. We were together for shorter periods of time at work.

Many couples work together, and they make it work because of mutual respect and love for each other. I believe it takes "give and take" and lots of patience. If working with your spouse is an option you're considering, keep in mind it requires mutual respect and lots of patience, trust, and a forgiving heart. And above all, each of you must give 100% to the relationship. There's no such thing as 50/50.

Once you figure it out, it's an unfair advantage to your competition. It's hard to find anyone more supportive and more trusting. Your spouse will always have your back. I know my husband cares about me, he cares about the company, and he cares about our clients.

Once I had Melissa and Claude on board, it was time to add another member of the family.

Our youngest daughter Crystal was 4-1/2 years old when I became a real estate agent. She would tell anyone who asked what she wanted to be when she grew up that she was going to be a REALTOR® like her mommy. But then she grew up and changed her mind several times (from physical therapist to marine biologist). Then one day when she was a senior, she told me, "I want to get my real estate license." We had expected her to go to college. She always loved school, and she had maintained an "A" average throughout high school. Because she had maintained an "A" average, she was allowed to take the real estate classes while still in high school. So Crystal became licensed as soon as she graduated. I knew Crystal would do very well in whatever she did. She had an outgoing personality, and she was an extremely mature 18-year-old.

So two years after Melissa had come on board, Crystal joined her sister, working together doing administrative duties and also both working as buyers' agents. And Claude spent most of his time on the road.

Even though we worked together, we weren't really seeing ourselves as a team. There were no teams back then. But in reality we were a team. Trainers across the country were just starting to talk about licensed assistants and non-licensed assistants.

Back then it was the four of us working together to better serve our clientele.

I was always searching for new ideas and for better ways to do a better job for our clients. I always felt it was important to be the leader of the pack and be first to offer new services or new technology.

It was 1998 when I saw an ad that caught my eye in our REALTOR® trade publication. It was a Craig Proctor Seminar. It was a three-day seminar in Toronto.

I discussed it with Claude, and we decided it would be worth our while to check it out. Flying for me at that time was not an option, so Claude, Crystal, and I took an eight-hour road trip to Toronto, while Melissa stayed behind to take care of the business.

There was lots of information, and the days were very long. We started at 7:30AM and did not end until 9:30 PM, with just two breaks.

I have to admit that I actually wanted to leave early a couple of times because I was totally exhausted, but Crystal talked me out of it. She was taking notes like there was no tomorrow. I smiled with pride seeing her genuine enthusiasm. I realized then that we shared the same familiar insatiable thirst for knowledge.

The trip was well worth our time. We came back with lots of products that would catapult our business to a new level.

We purchased Craig's website, a 24-hour hotline, and lots of printed material. The most exciting revelation that weekend was when Craig Proctor described "the office of the future." He was describing us – the four of us!

His presentation was that the team system was the office of the future. We looked at each other and smiled. We already had the team system – and we already had the office of the future. We only had to implement more systems.

We went to Toronto as me, the agent with three licensed assistants. We came back as a real estate team – a family team.

Always be on the lookout for learning opportunities. Always be curious about not only what other agents or real estate companies are doing, but be curious on how other industries operate their businesses.

No matter if you're a single agent, a team, or a broker/owner, you own your own business. You are the CEO of your own business when you're a real estate agent.

The Craig Proctor seminar opened up a whole new set of ideas and systems for us. We probably implemented half of what we learned that weekend. Some parts of it I didn't feel comfortable using. And that's O.K. Take what you believe will work for you – and leave the rest behind. Never stop learning.

It wasn't too long after that when I realized we were in need of a buyer agent on a full-time basis. When my husband was not running errands or putting up signs, he was showing homes for me on a part-time basis. And so were Melissa and Crystal, when needed. They had become mostly full-time administrators.

Crystal took charge of our new website and shared the listing paperwork with Melissa. They both helped me set up showings, and Melissa helped me coordinate closings.

One day during one of our early-morning walks, I brought up the idea of hiring a full-time buyer agent to Claude. His first question to me was, "How are we going to pay for this buyer agent?" I replied, "That buyer agent will pay for himself or herself."

I knew we had the buyers. And it was hard to keep up with the demand. Claude was working lots of nights and weekends. And I was also still showing property now and then. I truly believed we were ready for another team member.

Claude wasn't excited about the idea, but he had learned years earlier that once I came up with an idea and my decision was made, there was a slim chance he could talk me out of it. So he trusted my instincts and finally came on board.

My first instinct was to ask a young agent at our company by the name of Bob. He was always kind, considerate, friendly, and easy to co-broke with, so we asked if he might be interested in joining our team. We took him and his wife out to dinner one Friday night to discuss the opportunities in joining us as a buyer agent.

He accepted our offer, but quit before he even got started. I heard through the grapevine that he was worried he would have to work too many hours. So it wasn't meant to be. There was someone else out there that would become a better fit. I was convinced of that; I just didn't know who it was at the time. I believe this setback was a blessing in disguise and that everything happens for a reason. So we just kept searching.

Then Crystal mentioned her fiancé, Bill, as a possible candidate for a buyer agent. By this time, Crystal was 19, and Bill was 21. Bill was working at the service counter of NAPA Auto Parts, making minimum wage. Everyone there loved Billy. His boss loved him, and so did his co-workers and the customers.

Because he was so service oriented, all the NAPA customers flocked to Billy's service counter. He definitely had the personality, and I absolutely loved him too. I had been searching for an experienced agent, but then again, a new agent has no bad habits and you can train him or her yourself. So I began to see how it could really work.

What I didn't know at the time was that Bill was not convinced real estate was for him. Crystal had her work cut out for her. He did agree to meet with me to discuss the logistics.

I found out later that his parents were not convinced either. They had the same thought I had when the real estate idea was first introduced to me by my husband. Their thought was that it was a risk because the income was not steady. The idea of him leaving a "steady income" job for a "sales" job was a huge risk.

Bill did move forward with Crystal's encouragement and gave NAPA his two-week notice.

Bill became our first full-time buyer agent at the age of 21, and he became a top-notch real estate pro. But not without challenges.

If you ask Bill, he would tell you that his first few months in the business were pure hell for him. I just never knew this at the time. He absolutely hated real estate. He hated that he didn't know what he was doing. He was overwhelmed with everything he had to learn. He hated prospecting, but he did it anyway. He hated how customers and clients thought he was too young and used that against him. But he didn't give up. He just worked harder.

We had weekly training meetings with everyone on the team. He knew he had a lot to learn, and he was willing. He knew he had to prove himself. It took time, but he survived the challenges. He never gave up. He might have thought of quitting, but he never did. Today, he has an amazing following of loyal clients.

He's been a team member since 1999 and a top producer each and every year. He is very generous with his time, mentoring and training new and experienced agents on a continuous basis. He took extensive training on the national level, both as a buyer specialist and listing specialist, and came back to train our agents. He is a very gifted team leader and instructor.

Our business continued to grow, and just when we were wondering where our next buyer agent could possibly come from, a year later Clay was making comments about how burned out he was with the restaurant business. Working 75-80 hours a week, 7 days a week including holidays, was not ideal for a young family with a one-year-old. He thought about becoming a state health inspector.

We were ready for that second buyer agent at that point, so I suggested he join our team. We had a meeting, and he agreed to come on board.

What I remember most about those early years was how amazing Clay was at problem solving immediately. He was just a natural at focusing on the solution as opposed to focusing on the problem. So many people see problems as roadblocks with no way through them.

My two sons-in-law prospected every day. It never crossed their minds not to prospect. It was part of their job description, and they just accepted it. They just did it! They did it every single day! And it paid off for them and for the team.

Clay was so happy to get to go home at a decent hour that working 50-55 hours a week was a piece of cake for him.

Just like Bill, he had all the qualities that make a successful real estate professional. I'm sure Clay's degree in hotel/restaurant management helped jump-start his real estate career.

And our business still continued to grow, thanks to the team system and the shared values. This is a definite advantage to a family business – a family usually shares the same values.

A year later our biggest challenge was that Bill and Clay had little time to prospect. I was down to making about five calls a day for new business. I was concerned that sooner or later the pipeline would dry up. Most of our business had become inbound calls – buyers and past clients, and referrals for those ready to move. They needed to either buy or sell, or both. Past clients were recommending us to family and friends. Because we had gone the extra mile and because we gave the world-class service the clients deserve, the community was spreading the word about our commitment to helping homebuyers and homesellers get positive results.

When Melissa or Crystal would ask how they heard about us, this was the typical answer, repeated time and time again: "My friend told me to call The Fontaine Team. They tell me you're the best!" or "I had three different people tell me to call you guys." "They tell me if you really want to sell your home, call Fontaine."

"If you really want to find the right home, call Fontaine. They don't want to sell you any house; they want to sell you the house that's right for you!"

The loyalty of our community is absolutely amazing, and our family is forever grateful. That is why we are so committed to giving back to our community through several different fundraisers involving children, cancer, and other childhood illnesses. We raised over $8,000 in 2016 for Make-a-Wish Maine to grant a wish for a seriously ill Maine child. We have been fundraising for Make-a-Wish Maine since 2009.

You can have the same loyalty by always putting your *clients* first, not the paycheck. If anyone ever does have the paycheck as priority, a client can and will read right through it.

Work diligently for your clients like you have a million dollars in the bank already because it's not about you; it's about them.

Look out for their best interest, the same way you would for your mom, your sister, or your best friend.

Just when we were wondering how to fit in more prospecting, our daughter Angie (Melissa's twin sister) mentioned how unhappy she was at the bank where she was working. She felt unappreciated (a common complaint among many employees).

I told her she could come join the team with one condition. She would have to do what was necessary to get licensed. This way she could prospect for the team. She agreed. I knew if she prospected, she would get leads that would turn into appointments, and those appointments would eventually turn into closings. And again, she would end up paying for herself. So after being in banking for ten years, she gave up her leadership position to join the family business. She gave her employer her two-week notice and signed up for the next real estate course. So now we would have all three daughters involved in the family business. It was 2001.

She was a natural. She has a great enthusiastic personality and telephone voice, which helps tremendously.

She called 2-3 hours a day. She immediately generated leads for the team. When she wasn't prospecting, she was setting up showings, giving seller feedback, and generating monthly sellers' reports that would be either e-mailed or mailed (depending on whether sellers had e-mail or not.)

I was proud of how quickly she picked up on the prospecting. I guess listening to her mom prospecting all those nights gave her a jump-start. (Hee-Hee!)

Each and every one of our family members had worked for a non-related employer. I don't think it's a good idea to hire a family member who has never worked anywhere else. I believe it makes them appreciate the real estate business and the family team more because they have a point of reference.

Unfortunately, hiring family members doesn't always work out. Be careful in your choices of who you bring on your team. Maybe you're thinking of hiring or recruiting your very best friend. Think long and hard. You always take that chance of destroying that friendship. If the business relationship doesn't work out, no matter what you decide to do, you must set rules right from the beginning.

If you decide to take your son on board, as an example, you must not be a micromanager. Remember you are his mentor. His success, in part, will depend on how you treat him, how much patience you have, and if you can put your ego aside and say "I'm sorry" when you slip up. We are all human and we all make mistakes; we have good intentions, but sometimes our emotions get in the way. Apologize and move forward. It's so worth it!

Believe me, I have said "I'm sorry" to my daughters and sons-in-law many times, and they also have said "I'm sorry" to me, and then we move on.

When I was growing up, my mom would never ever say she was sorry. She did finally toward the end of her life. So much time was wasted because she couldn't say those two little words to take responsibility. When you know you may have overreacted, set the example.

Over time we did hire outside the family, but because the name of our company is Fontaine Family – The Real Estate Leader, many people assume everyone is family and that we just don't hire outside of family. But we do, and we have for 12 years now.

Recently I noticed on Facebook that a past client's daughter had just passed her real estate exam, so I private messaged her to ask if she had made a commitment yet. I went on to say that I would love to chat with her about joining our team. I already knew she had had success in sales. The first thing she said was how honored she was and that she didn't realize we hired outside the family.

So we met soon after, and she joined us immediately. I know her mom and dad, and I know we share the same values. Everything else you can train, but you can't train people on values. And you can't train people to be nice. They either have good moral values or they don't. They are either nice or they're not.

You never know where your next recruit will come from.

At the beginning of building my team, I would just ask my agents if they knew anyone who would be a good fit, and I would interview them. And then decide from there.

Always do your due diligence. Then just trust your instincts; listen to your heart.

Maybe you're a single agent now, but it's a big step. Just take a baby step and hire someone for a few hours a week, like I did. Four hours a week is a very small step, but it worked. You can keep increasing the hours as needed. It's so much easier to make the decision when it's done in small increments.

Build the team slowly rather than fast. I have seen many agents build teams that went down like a house of cards. Grow slow and steady, and you will have a solid foundation.

TOP FIVE LESSONS FROM CREATING THE FAMILY BUSINESS

1. Don't be afraid to implement new ideas and concepts to grow your business.

2. Take the time to build your team with the right individuals.

3. Temperament, personality and human relations skills are the most important "people" skills for your team.

4. Treat your clients like you would treat your family.

5. Trust your team members to make good decisions for the team... you can't do it all!

"Leaders Should Strive for Authenticity over Perfection."

Sheryl Sandberg

Facebook COO

CHAPTER 4

LEADERSHIP IS LIKE BEING
A GOOD MOTHER

never had any formal leadership training, and learned about that important characteristic mostly through my experience and by happenstance.

I know for sure that having started the team with family members is what created our culture of treating our team members and our clients like family. I believe that my parenting skills have helped in my leadership skills. Leading a team is a lot like leading a family. You need to care for them, keep them safe, and look out for them.

Once we started hiring and recruiting outside of the family, I was determined that we would treat those team members as an extended family. We want our workplace to be a fun place to be where everyone cares about each other – and that starts at the top. It starts with the leader or leaders.

I see myself as the coach who encourages each member of the family team to be the best they can be. We celebrate together, we learn together, we play together.

I believe we all learn leadership at a young age. It starts with our parents. Even though my mom had flaws and she struggled through life with alcoholism, she had leadership qualities that I didn't recognize for many years. I can still hear her voice in my head say, "Brenda, you can be whatever you want to be in life. Follow your dreams." And my dad had great sound advice throughout my childhood. "Do what's right. Do what you say you're going to do. Trust is everything, so always keep your word."

In order for me to be the best leader possible, I continue to study the market, the new technology available, etc., always striving to be on the cutting edge. We were the first in our company at ERA to get a website, the first to get a moving van. We were the first in Maine to get a mobile website. And, of course, we were the first in our area to build a real estate team.

I take my leadership role very seriously. I am leading a powerhouse team, and I know it's a big responsibility.

I also know how important it is to show appreciation, to praise and to recognize our team members. No one can ever get enough praise. We celebrate our victories as a team, and we share our challenges with each other. We help each other solve problems by focusing on the solutions.

As a leader, continuous training is a priority. We currently have five trainers, including myself, who are training our agents, new and experienced, on a weekly basis. Our team meetings are training meetings. And I know this will be a priority for the future generations.

Our professionalism is of the utmost importance. And we strive to be the trailblazers.

We also strive to be the most highly skilled real estate professionals – and that means we are not and never will be happy with status quo.

It takes lots of commitment to always be researching the best marketing ideas available out there for our clients. But we know how much our future business depends on us keeping ahead of the competition. A lot of what we do at Fontaine Team stems from what I experienced at ERA.

Tim was always generous with recognizing and praising his agents. We always had amazing and fun awards banquets. We also planned fun skits where we would practice weeks in advance. What great team bonding! We had contests where agents would receive prizes at the end of the contest for most sales. Very motivating! Loved the prizes!

We always had wall boards with agents' names and production – again very motivating. We had weekly meetings, summer outings, Christmas parties. We were like family!

I adopted every one of those traditions for The Fontaine Family Team.

Today, unfortunately for many agents, the majority of owners are from out of state, and the agent is just one of many agents. It's very corporate.

It makes a difference when the owner is not "in the store" on a weekly basis – a huge difference. It shows in the office environment, the culture, and the production. Agents need to know that you have their backs, that you care, and that you're not just a number. Our agents matter; our support staff matters.

I have spoken to several agents who joined our team that were previously with a large company. It's interesting how they repeat the same sentiment. They felt like just a number. They felt isolated and very much alone.

They have found us to be on the total opposite of the spectrum – and they love it! They love being part of the family. It's a totally different culture. It's more about daily sharing of ideas, success stories, challenges, and helping each other succeed. And that's what a family does. Everyone supports each other and is happy for each other's success. We love having fun together too! And do we ever!

I am truly grateful for the part that Tim played in helping me succeed. And I hope that someday someone can say that about me.

Because I pride myself on being a lifelong learner, it's not a surprise to me that many different people have influenced my leadership skills. You can learn so much from other leaders – and not just in the real estate industry. I enjoy studying business leaders and really appreciate what they have to offer. I love Tony Robbins, Jim Rohn, Darren Hardy, to name a few. As far as real estate coaches and trainers, we love Brian Buffini. He fits our culture. He is all about relationships – creating client relationships for life. So keep your eyes and ears open to everything and everyone. They all have something to offer.

Tim was an excellent leader. I admire and appreciate him even more now than I did before becoming a leader and broker/ owner. He helped me along this real estate journey, and I will always be grateful. I made many mistakes along the way, but he helped me work things out.

He also had some difficult decisions to make that I should have appreciated more at the time. I wish I had known then what I know now. It's not easy to tell an agent, "It's time for you to leave." I always respected him, but now that I have walked in those same shoes, I respect him even more.

It's not easy. Tim made it look easy. It's freakin' hard!! Some days are more difficult than others. But when there is conflict and people don't get along, someone has to go. This is a difficult story for me to tell, but here goes.

There was a top-producing agent that had come on board the ERA agency. I had been with ERA for about ten years at that point. This man lived to make my life miserable. He was mean-spirited and tried very hard to put everyone against me. He called me names I can't repeat and wished me stomach cancer. (Little did he know that my dad had died of stomach cancer, which made it even more hurtful.)

There's more, but I think you get the picture. Anyway, he was very abusive. Some days he could flip it around completely, and act like he wanted to be my best friend. And the next day, he was back at it.

I know he didn't have respect for any woman. You just had to observe how he treated his wife (she was an agent too), and he hated me because I was selling more than he was. He wanted to be top dog. He had been the top producer at his previous agency, and it was too big of a pill to swallow to be #2; he was truly trying to push me out. He had a big ego! It went on for months and I finally told Tim. We had a meeting with the bully – me, Tim, and also Dave, our sales manager. He apologized, but nothing changed. He would be very nice with people around, but if he caught me alone, he would attack me with his filthy mouth of abusive words.

I didn't want to go back to Tim right away, so I asked my husband for advice. He said, "Let me talk to him!" I had told my husband very little about it because I knew he would be furious, but I felt it was time. My husband was not in the office much, but he made a point to go in when the bully would be there. My husband told me that he completely denied any wrongdoing. I don't know why I expected anything different.

So I just couldn't take it anymore. This was my third complaint to Tim. He needed to leave, or I would have to leave.

Tim actually told me that he found himself driving past the office when he would see the bully's car in the parking lot. He just couldn't deal with all his "stuff" either.

Tim would tell him he had to go the next day. Tim told me not to come to the office at all and to stay away from the area for the whole day.

If Tim only knew how scared I was of this man! I actually feared for my life. I had visions of him coming to my house, breaking in, and stabbing me for having him fired. And then he would deny he ever went to my house, and he would get away with murder. Yes, it had played all out in my head. I know now how irrational I was being. But "my skeletons in my closet" come out occasionally when I'm under a lot of stress.

So Tim did call him into his office, and told him he had to leave. We heard later that when he left Tim, he immediately went down the street to the next closest real estate company and was hired on the spot.

I was so relieved when I heard the news. My life was normal again. And the whole office was happy the bully was gone.

Have you ever been bullied or know someone who has been? So many people have experienced it. And it seems to be getting worse – for so many people of all ages.

What's different today is the young teens and young adults that are bullied get it 24/7 because of social media. Imagine constant bullying. Everyone must stand up to these bullies. We must push through our fears and let the people in charge know what's going on. No one deserves to be called names. No one deserves to be isolated. No one should be made to feel unworthy. Let's expose all the bullies. What is sad is that sometimes – not always, but sometimes – the parent is a bully too. Where do you think the child learned it from? Maybe it wasn't a parent, but it's possible he/she learned the behavior from someone he/she knows. The child may have been a victim himself or herself.

The lesson I learned from this experience is to push through my fear again and expose the bully, even though I feared for my life. It was my perception. But it felt real to me.

Going through challenging situations helped prepare me for the difficult time to come for our family business.

The market downturn of 2008 created many sleepless nights. We quickly needed to cut expenses. Our largest expense was wages. All real estate companies and teams were feeling the crises. Some companies merged, some disappeared.

Our sales dropped by 30%. We had been toying with the idea of going out on our own as an independent company or maybe joining another franchise. We put that decision on hold while we figured out what we could do to survive this downturn.

I researched how to get some of the REO business (bank foreclosures). We found out it was all about offering free BPO's (broker's price opinions) and eventually we could possibly get a few listings. We have never been afraid of hard work, so we were up for the task. My daughter Crystal assisted me in this endeavor (Crystal deserves much credit for the growth of this segment of our business), and within six months the hard work started paying off. It was helping to pay the bills, but we still needed to cut expenses. We had five licensed support staff at the time. That's a big payroll to meet every week when business is slow. The first thing we did was to cut both my salary and my husband's by 25%. We then had a meeting with our staff and shared with them that we had to cut expenses. So when we asked our employees to accept a minor reduction, we told them we had taken the first cut. Leaders must always lead by example. But that was still not enough.

So whom do you lay off? There was less work to do, so someone had to leave – or did they? Three of our staff members are our daughters, two are not.

We had a family meeting, and we decided to do what we had been doing from the beginning – treat everyone like family. What would be the right thing to do? We would cut everyone's hours equally. Everyone would take a hit so no one would get laid off. By having each team member cut eight hours (8 x 5 = 40 hours), it would be like laying off one employee without laying off anyone. Everyone agreed, and it worked out beautifully. And we survived the downturn!

Because of our family culture, our team is always helping one another and expecting nothing in return. We have a generous and caring team who really love each other and are committed to each other's well-being. We are family in every sense of the word.

That's what makes it difficult when you have to say "goodbye" to a member of the team.

I get extremely close to my team members, and so does the whole family. There does come a time when a team member feels it's their turn to lead and take the same steps toward growth that I did.

It's hard to see them go, but I do see it as a positive reflection on our leadership. We have grown another leader! We are happy, but it's always bittersweet. We maintain the relationship and wish them well. We have had others leave because they didn't like to see us grow. We must choose growth or we would die like others have.

When all your agents are busy with appointments and they struggle to find more time in their day for new business, you know it's time to hire more agents. So you have no choice; you either grow or you give poor service and die quickly.

When we started recruiting aggressively, a couple of agents didn't like it and left. It was hard to see them go, but over time, we realized everything happens for a reason. And again, with adversity comes blessings.

Since the change, our business has increased both in sales volume and closed units.

So you can't worry about agents leaving. If they're not happy, you really don't want them in the office complaining. It brings everyone down. And we did have a short period where we had negativity because of one agent.

As soon as that agent left, it was like a cloud lifted and the sunshine returned – and we were back to that happy place once again!

We've always led with a positive and enthusiastic attitude. We are one big happy family again. Your work environment should be a fun place! You should look forward to walking in your office every day with happy faces welcoming you with a warm smile and an enthusiastic "Good Morning!"

When you are a leader, expect loyalty from your agents. When I was working at ERA and I knew someone was unhappy about something, I would go to Tim and just say, "You may want to talk to this agent." It is so important to have open communication. Sometimes the agent may not want to go directly to the broker/owner so they just complain to someone else in hopes it will get to the owner, and so the owner approaches them.

My team members know they can go to my sons-in-law, Bill or Clay, or my daughters, Melissa, Angie, or Crystal, about anything if they don't want to come directly to me.

Everyone on the team is very important. No one is more important than the other – not me – no one!

Stay humble. Remember where you came from. Treat everyone with respect and kindness even when it is difficult. I'm not saying to be a doormat. You definitely have to stand up for yourself. You shouldn't ever allow anyone to verbally abuse you.

But if things are not going your way, don't abuse your vendors. I have overheard many agents over the years (when I was a single agent) verbally abuse appraisers, lenders, loan processors, closing agents, building inspectors, and co-broking agents. It's amazing how much progress you can make when you strive for a win-win. Also remember those vendors could be your future clients.

Today I have given up some of the leadership roles in the family business to the second generation.

I still conduct the weekly meetings in both locations – Auburn, Maine and Scarborough, Maine – and I continue to train and help new agents problem solve. I am also consistently researching for new ways to better serve our clients. Melissa is our office manager. I have set it up so the agents can go to her first. Most agents go to her first with transaction problems, and she still is our closing coordinator and short sale specialist. She also has authority to sign checks, and the agents can still get paid when Claude and I are on vacation. I do a lot of the training, but we also have Bill, Clayton, and Karen (and Marie has trained new staff members too). Bill is also our team leader; he handles agent issues. Clay is my sounding board for management and problem solving. Both Bill and Clay conduct meetings when I'm not available.

So our team is well prepared for the future. My responsibility as a leader is to be a good resource for all team members. I love my team; I love adding value to each of them by inspiring them to grow and go beyond their comfort zone, like I did. I truly listen and try to understand their challenges, and I focus on their strengths and I share with them what I see. I don't make promises I can't keep. The hardest thing as a leader is letting go. Both Bill and Clay have natural leadership qualities. Since Bill is also a fire fighter, he has a knack for teaching, and Clay managed a restaurant. And my three daughters have watched me lead the majority of their lives, so they are well prepared.

Always do the right thing for your agents, and they'll do the right thing for their clients.

I'm not perfect. I definitely have made many mistakes (like hiring the wrong people), but I have learned from my mistakes. I've also learned not to react but to respond calmly (not easy, but doable). I really don't see leadership as a position of power. I see it as an opportunity to make a difference in the lives of our agents by inspiring them to be as successful as they want to be. It is extremely rewarding. I'm absolutely passionate about it!

I'm so blessed to have a career that is so gratifying and so much fun! There is really nothing else I would rather do. Because of my developing leadership, I was able to make the next tough decision for our team.

TOP FIVE LESSONS ON LEADERSHIP

1. However you keep notes – on your phone, on a pad or in your head – always take something away from people you work with that you can use for your team.

2. Lead by example, not by authority.

3. A great leader makes the other members of the team great as well.

4. Great leaders surround themselves with great team members. A team is only as strong as its weakest link.

5. You're not a leader just because your title says you are.

"If You Put Everything Off till You're Sure of It, You'll Get Nothing Done."

Norman Vincent Peale

Author
The Power of Positive Thinking

CHAPTER 5

THE TEAM MAKES A MOVE

I didn't wake up one day and just think, "We need to move location." I was actually inspired to do it after leaving a closing. The closing was held in an older home in a corner of a living room where a small kitchen table had been placed. The broker/owner used a part of her home as her real estate agency.

I left there thinking if this real estate broker can have her own space, why can't we? So I left there on the hunt for our own space. I was not thinking of leaving ERA. We just needed more space. Our supplies were taking over the back stairway. And we were already cramped because we had just adopted our first nonfamily team member.

Two years earlier Tim had built a huge addition, and Fontaine Team occupied the whole second floor. And previously Tim had been extremely gracious to give up his own office for us because we had outgrown our space back then. It had started with just me, Claude, Melissa, and Crystal. But then came Bill and Clay, and later on Angie joined too.

We were in Tim's office space for about four years. Now just two years later, we were running out of space again. Well, that same afternoon I found a great location on Center Street in

Auburn. It was only about 1,000 feet from ERA's main office. This was going to work great because we would still be making several trips to ERA for closing files, earnest money, and picking up our checks. There was over 2,300 square feet of office space and plenty of parking.

I took the family to see it. The girls were a little nervous. Bill and Clay were totally on board, as well as Claude. I did tell my broker/owner Tim right away. I asked him if he would like to see it, and he did. But he didn't have much to say. I'm sure he was seeing the writing on the wall and that it was just a matter of time. I made it clear that we were making a physical move, but we weren't leaving the company. And one more baby step was made.

The transition was easier than expected. All the desks, computers, and file cabinets were ours. We just needed conference tables and chairs, a phone system, a server, and exterior signage. And in order to make a good first impression, we had a massive customized reception desk built to allow room for two receptionists to sit out front for future training purposes. My husband often says that I always "overthink" everything. Sometimes it pays off.

Once we settled in, we all knew that it was the right decision. It was 2004.

Many people thought then that we had left ERA, even though *ERA Worden* was still on our signs. We did have a prominent Fontaine logo. Tim approved our signs, and we were on our way to more amazing growth.

As I mentioned earlier, we had just taken on our first nonfamily member. She had heard we were looking to hire outside the family for the first time, and I will never forget the day she approached me. She was unhappy with her team leader. She felt unappreciated. One of the incidents that upset her the most was the day her team leader approached me, with her alongside, and actually tried to "rent" her out to me. (That was a very uncomfortable and awkward moment.) I just told her team leader it wouldn't work. Imagine how that buyer agent felt. She told me (after she joined our team) that she felt her leader thought of her more like a commodity than a human being.

I called the team leader before bringing her on board, and was very honest about her buyer agent approaching me about joining our team. She took it well and felt she didn't want someone on her team that was not happy.

So we took the buyer agent on quickly because we all had known her for years working at ERA; we all loved her, and she loved our whole family too. In fact, when she joined us, she said, and I quote, "I feel like I just won the lottery!" It proved to be a smart decision.

As soon as we moved location, I received a call from the receptionist at a title company inquiring if we were hiring a receptionist.

I knew her well because most of our closings were held at this title company. She was always extremely friendly and welcoming whenever I went in for a closing. I was always impressed with her positive attitude and warm smile.

I told Marie we would not be ready to hire another staff member for six months, but that we would love to have her join the team. She had been working there for over eight years, so I knew she had to be a good employee, and she has proven that decision to be correct. But it was after her hire that we had to make another challenging decision.

Five years flew by, and as I wrote earlier, we survived the financial crisis of 2008. But after that bad year, I knew we needed to "cut the cord" because we were paying franchise fees in the six figures. It was one of the most difficult decisions I have ever had to make.

I had been approached by a franchise for several years. They had even paid for Claude and me to attend their annual convention (all expenses paid). I was impressed with their culture because it was similar to ours. We thought we had decided to do it, and then my gut was telling me to do more due diligence – you know, that inner voice you hear when it's a very difficult decision. So I called two broker/owners who had previously been with the franchise. I wanted to know why they had left. The first one I met told me she was tired of being constantly pushed to recruit when she was perfectly happy with the amount of agents she had in her company. The second broker/owner told me the exact same thing.

I was starting to have "buyer's remorse." I was expecting a call from the CEO of the franchise, so I decided to wait and to listen to what he had to say. There's no doubt he is a brilliant man, and I really liked him. But when I told him I was not interested in recruiting 100 agents and that I believed in quality rather than quantity, he really had no comment. I went on to say, "Largest doesn't necessarily mean best!" Surprisingly, he agreed. So we decided that this franchise or any franchise was not the right fit for us, because our goal wasn't and never will be to be the largest. Our goal is to give the best customer service with the best trained and highly skilled quality agents, and always put the interest of our clients first.

I called Tim Worden and asked to meet with him. I felt telling him in person was the right thing to do. At first he thought we were leaving to go to another franchise because he knew I had been talking to one in particular. I was always upfront about everything. He did surprise me when he said, "If you join that franchise, it's going to be like you are piercing a knife through my heart!" I will never forget those words. With a lump in my throat, I sadly replied, "No, I'm not joining them or anyone else."

So we picked the date that we would make the transition. I'm sure Tim had been expecting it for years, especially after we moved out. It had taken us five years to make the big decision of going out on our own.

The day after I broke the news, I wrote a heartfelt letter to Tim and company. I shared with everyone that it had been a difficult decision and how hard it was to leave. I also added that we really appreciated each and every one of them and how much we would miss them all. But we had great memories that would never be forgotten.

And while I was expressing my feelings on paper, the tears were coming down like raindrops, staining my draft.

It was a very emotional day, one of several reasons why I had put it off for so long. I knew it would be emotionally draining.

The date we picked was May 11. We were about 30 days away, and my staff had a lot of work to do. I found out later that my daughters were going into the office each day at 4 AM the week of the transition (without my knowledge). We had over 200 listings. If we ever decided to leave, Tim and I had an agreement in writing that clients could decide if they wanted to follow The Fontaine Team or stay with ERA. And we had permission to contact the clients and ask them what they wanted to do. 99.9% chose to stay with us.

Our staff was amazing. They got all the work done seamlessly.

My fear was that we could lose 100 or more listings. I had put a lot of value on the ERA franchise because of my 25 years of emotional connection, but our clients didn't care. Again, my fears were unfounded. Our clients were perfectly happy with us being independent. We have found that the community loves working and supporting local businesses.

More franchises called and wanted to meet, but we had already decided to stay independent based on our clients' feedback. We really didn't need franchises. I knew that, but I had been worried about public perception.

We always kept and continue to keep our website fresh, and it is always ranked one of the top real estate sites in the country. We had our systems in place, as well as our training, so there was no need for a franchise.

The month after we went on our own, the business next door to us in our strip mall closed. I saw this as an opportunity for us. All we had to do was open up one wall, and we would gain about 1,000 square feet. We were able to negotiate a lower rate. So we took over that commercial space, which gave us more room to grow.

After we left the franchise, I immediately began my search for national training. That's when I found Brian Buffini. It was 2009. I immediately signed up for his systems and became a certified mentor for his Peak Producer program. Our team meetings were longer than usual with the Peak Producer program, but we had 100% attendance for all 12 weeks. Everyone enjoyed it, and it fit our culture perfectly. Brian believes in creating lifelong client relationships, and he teaches a systemized approach. I also was involved in his coaching program and have been attending his MasterMind Summits – and it's absolutely life changing!

So on May 11, 2009, Fontaine Family Team was a licensed agency and became Fontaine Family – The Real Estate Leader. I know it was the best decision we could have ever made. This would mean, however, more changes for me.

As soon as we had two buyer agents, I was able to just concentrate on the listing side of the business. It's important to know that your ability to grow will depend on how well or how willing you are to delegate. I am not a control freak, but I have had times where I found it difficult letting go of certain parts of the business. Again, it's all about taking baby steps.

Even at the beginning, I had a hard time giving up the ad writing on my listings. Then I decided to start asking my sellers what they loved about their homes. What was it that swayed them to buy it? The sellers' answers became the ad. I would ask them to name ten things that they absolutely loved about their homes. The sellers loved having input, and they loved the ads and the remarks because they were in their own words. We continue to use this system today.

I guess I hated delegating ad writing because I always enjoyed writing. But it was necessary to allow me to do other things. There comes a time in your business that you must pick your priorities, and some parts of the business need to be delegated. Once you start delegating, you will find that there are some things that others can do better than you. And that's why the team system works so well.

Once I stopped working with buyers, I had more time to research new marketing ideas, take listings, counsel my seller clients, study the market, and train new team members.

The very hardest piece to let go was taking listings. In order to have time to train, conduct meetings, recruit, help problem solve, and continue to work on the business to stay on the cutting edge, I had to slowly wean myself. So any new calls to list were passed out to our experienced agents. And I continued to list my past clients only.

Then, with the help of my Buffini coach, I gave up the listing side of the business completely (except for the bank-owned properties).

My coach helped me on how to explain it to my past clients and also to those who had been referred. I still get calls today where they just want to talk to me, and I still answer every one of the calls, explaining that our family business has led me in a different direction. Due to our growth, I no longer list property or work with buyers. I really must be focused on the management and training part of the business. I'm also constantly researching for new and better tools to market our listings.

I typically say, "I will get you connected to one of our top-notch agents who will take great care of you. If, for any reason, you have any questions or concerns at any time, don't hesitate to pick up the phone and call me. I'm here for you."

I always make myself available for all our clients. I know it's important for me to be easily accessible. Our clients are very important to me and to all of us.

It was actually very difficult to let go of the listing side. I loved it so much.

Today, I have become very passionate about helping our agents become successful. So after delegating the listing side, my daughter Crystal (our Lead Coordinator) takes care of coordinating our listing leads so we continue to respond quickly. We must always remain true to our mission.

FONTAINE FAMILY TEAM MISSION

We strive to give our clients world-class service by going above and beyond the call of duty, thus creating raving fans who will enthusiastically recommend us to their family and friends. Our goal is to obtain the highest level of customer satisfaction because our future business depends on it.

After we survived 2008, things started to take off for the team, and 2009-2014 were our growth years. Our world-class service was creating raving fans. And these raving fans were spreading the word about their positive experience with The Fontaine Team. The Fontaine Team continued to be known as the name family and friends recommend. We also started working with the second generation – the adult children of my past clients. It's so gratifying to be working with all the family members. This is what having clients for life is all about. We were growing our customer base and our sales were increasing dramatically, but I had not yet focused on recruiting.

We kept our team to 10-11 agents plus a staff of five until 2010, when we hired Karen, our sixth staff member, as our marketing director. She was a great hire because she already had eight years of real estate experience. Eventually she obtained her Broker's license and became one of our designees.

Recruiting was not a focus during this time. Agents from other teams or other agencies were calling me, asking to join the team. Sometimes the timing was right because one of our agents had moved out of state or one had decided on changing careers. Then I would agree to meet for an interview.

It wasn't until 2014 that I decided to make recruiting a focus. But back then I still wanted to keep the sales agents to 10-12.

Many times throughout this story you've heard me emphasize how important it is to your business to cultivate and maintain great clients. I try to not only say this, but to show it in every reasonable way.

In 2013 I was celebrating 30 years in real estate. We decided to have a special event honoring our top 200 clients who had repeatedly hired us and recommended us over the years. We chose a beautiful historic venue, "The Royal Oak Room" in Lewiston. We had hors d'oeuvres served and had live music. The theme of the event was celebrating the clients for their loyalty. To show our appreciation and to make our clients feel special, we rolled out a "Fontaine blue" carpet and photographed each client in front of a media backdrop banner (just like the movie stars). Each one of our honored guests received their picture in the mail with a thank you note. We also had gifts placed at each of their reserved seats.

We started the evening with me going up to say a few words to express our gratitude for their loyalty. It turned out to be a great success. Everyone had a great time and it was a memorable life event.

I remember one of our guests coming up to me and saying, "Brenda, I'm so impressed. I see people here from every walk of life. That says so much about you and your family." I just smiled and said, "Thank you." I never would have thought of inviting guests just based on their status in the community. It was totally based on our client relationships, and not on how much money they made or what they did for a living.

I will never forget where I came from; I am still the same person, and I always will be.

Once again, it was time for a big move for Fontaine Team. For many years we have taken the week of the Fourth of July to enjoy family time camping near the ocean. My sons-in-law Bill and Clay had mentioned several times how we should have an office in the Greater Portland area. I would dismiss the idea by responding that real estate in that area was out of our reach. If we would get a second location, we would want to purchase the real estate.

So we were camping in the Old Orchard Beach area, and we were walking out of a restaurant when we bumped into a Portland REALTOR®.

He was surprised to see us in the area, and he was excited to share his great news that he had just taken a deposit on a million dollar home. I congratulated him and said, "Wow, that's great. Maybe we should open an office in this area."

I was surprised at myself for having said that out loud. I was repeating what I had heard Bill and Clay say for a few years. But it never seemed to be the right time. I would just say, "Someday we will." But someday never comes. When you think it is not the right time, you wonder, is there ever a perfect time? When do you really know?

After my husband and I got in the car, I looked over at him and said, "Why not?" He said, "Why not what?" I said, "I think we should look for a second location. Why wait?"

So on that rainy Fourth of July in 2014, I convinced my husband we had nothing better to do than to drive up Route One from Saco to Cumberland in search of a modest two-story building with a paved parking lot.

We did not find anything that day, but now that I had actually said it out loud, I was on a mission. I was not going to give up the search. Our sons-in-law had talked about it for years, but it was such a huge step. It was another step out of the comfort zone, but this was no baby step. This was a huge leap of faith. The search was on.

After an MLS (Multiple Listing System) search, a few options came up. The one that really caught my eye was 432 US Route One in Scarborough, a two-story gambrel style home with paved parking for twelve cars. My husband and I scheduled a showing with the listing agent. The location was perfect, but the building needed a lot of work. The listing agent shared with us some interesting history; one of the facts was that the building had been built originally for a real estate office!

We scheduled another appointment a week later to show it to the rest of the family. I had checked the days on market and asked the agent why he thought it had been on the market so long. We found out that the previous tenant had tried to get financing for two years. The owner had given him extra time because his wife was seriously ill and passed away. It was a very sad story.

Crystal and Bill felt it was a great investment. Clay liked the idea and the location, but thought we might be five years away from making such a big step. Melissa and Angie were apprehensive but stayed neutral.

For two months I kept thinking about the space and what a great opportunity and what a great location it was. We were selling property in Old Orchard Beach, Saco, Portland, etc., but few people knew that. Our buyer agents were selling these properties, but most of the public had no idea. We needed to let the Greater Portland Area know we were doing business in this community.

I truly believed that having a brick-and-mortar location was the best way to have presence in the community.

I called every few weeks to get an update on the activity and to see if the agent had leased the space yet, because it was for sale and for lease. When I called in September, he informed me that buyers from Florida were coming to see it for the second time. My heart sank. I told my husband it was time for us to make a decision. I am very fortunate that my husband usually takes my lead. He knows when my mind is made up, it's hard to change it.

I let the whole family know we were going to make an offer and that I believed we needed to at least try. So we went ahead and made the offer. We negotiated back and forth, and finally agreed on a price. After the inspections, we renegotiated.

I have to share with you that I prayed for guidance throughout this whole process. I believed that if it wasn't meant to be, roadblocks would appear. There was no major roadblock. It was a very smooth transaction, and we closed two weeks later. The remodeling project took two and a half months.

We held our grand opening on February 12, 2015. We had invited 75 people (agents, vendors, friends, family) and had a great turnout. One of our past clients and family member of one of our team members agreed to perform a short skit for us. So comedian Bob Marley came with his family and helped with the ribbon cutting and later entertained us with his Maine humor. We adore him. We will be forever grateful to Bob and also to Pat, our team member, for helping to make the event special.

We opened our second location with no receptionist and no local agents. Our Auburn staff rotated daily until we could find someone we trusted. Four of our Auburn agents volunteered to work both locations.

My first receptionist was awesome, but she moved to Florida after working with us for five months. Our second receptionist didn't understand the work. We kept her longer than we should have. I wanted to get feedback from a few agents, so I asked them to rate her on a scale from 1-10. They rated her a 7. I thought that might be good for some places, but we needed better than that, and I also wondered if they might have been generous. What was amazing is the two agents I asked gave me the same rating. I finally told her the first week of January that it wasn't working out and that I would give her a severance pay – I wanted her to leave on good terms.

We put an ad on the internet and received 75 resumes – that was overwhelming! I put Melissa and Crystal in charge of reviewing the resumes, and they took the best seven. I interviewed them on the phone and met with four. The best fit was an associate broker with a wonderful personality. I fell in love with Maryanne immediately, and she has been such a blessing. She is our Scarborough Listing Manager and Marketing Director, and has all the credentials to be an Office Manager since she has five years of real estate experience.

As far as recruiting is concerned, the intention I set was to recruit ten agents in the first year. And we have reached that goal. I do have space for two more agents. It's amazing what can be accomplished when you set out to reach a specific goal.

Even if you only have fifteen minutes a day to make calls – whether it's for listings, buyers, or agents – when you do it daily, it adds up to positive results. Unfortunately, what you might see as a positive move is sometimes viewed as a negative one by members of your team. That can be a difficult situation to navigate.

When we purchased the Scarborough property, it was a huge step for us. That was not a baby step! After that huge step, we had a team meeting to discuss our plan for growing and expanding into the Scarborough area. A few of the agents did not like the idea of us growing. The majority were on board, however, and saw it as a positive for all of us. Some people don't like change; they want everything to stay the same. So we had four leave – and we only had ten agents. I was devastated. There were many sleepless nights, but I put my faith in God and completely left it all in His hands. I knew it would all work out. I believed that better days were ahead.

Looking back, I realize that it was for the best for them as well as for The Fontaine Team. What it did was force me to learn how to recruit. I had never needed to know how before because the agents always came to me.

So I didn't just need to recruit for the Scarborough location, but now I had to rebuild the Auburn location too.

Amazingly, we finished the year of adversities with over $60 million in sales and 389 closings in 2015. We actually also expanded into the Augusta community by recruiting three seasoned agents in that area. They are doing great!

Today we have 18 agents in Auburn and 10 in Scarborough, and 7 licensed support staff who take care of agents in both locations.

Every one of our team members is very happy with the two locations, because it has increased their business. Our two locations can be utilized by every agent on our team. And it's happening more frequently as time goes on.

Even though we are in two locations, we are still one unified team. It's important to stay as one.

Everyone is eager to help one another, and that's what makes us such a powerhouse team. Our powerhouse team will exceed expectations and reach a new milestone by closing between 535-550 properties in 2016.

When I look back at our growth over the years and the success we have been so blessed to experience, one of the things that I believe made the difference is having the courage and the faith to take those baby steps. You must recognize the signs that it's time, and move forward. But I believe what got me through the toughest times was my faith in God. Without Him nothing is possible. With Him, anything is possible.

You might wonder why it took nearly 25 years to leave ERA. The truth is that I had seen several very successful agents leave their companies to go on their own and fail, then rejoin the company that they had left. I have always made a practice of learning from other people's mistakes.

So what I did was build our future company within the agency I was with. When we left ERA, we were doing 51% of the business. Could we have left earlier? Maybe. But no one will ever know for sure. I don't regret staying there all those years. I want to believe I made the right decisions.

We will be celebrating two years in Scarborough in a few months, and we're happy with the big leap of faith that we made because we are exceeding expectations. I know for sure that the decision to expand was a smart one.

I continue to spend two mornings a week in Scarborough and 2-3 mornings a week in Auburn.

I spend my afternoons by the lake in the summer reading business books or listening to podcasts. It's what I must do – to continuously focus on ways to add value and also to stay focused on our team mission. In the winter months, we take a couple of two-week vacations and several three- or four-day weekend trips to watch our grandkids play hockey. My husband and I have no worry about the family business. We know that it is in good hands...

...Not only because of the awesome team that we've built, but because of the one important ingredient that I've repeatedly told you about throughout our story.

FIVE LESSONS LEARNED FROM CONTINUOUS IMPROVEMENT

1. Growth isn't always a smooth transition.

2. Not everyone on the team will agree with your decisions... and that's okay.

3. Always communicate with your team when you're considering substantial changes to the business – it eliminates surprises.

4. When you remain consistent in the manner in which you treat people, both on your team and your clients, transitions have a way of working out well for all.

5. The great leader doesn't micromanage every aspect of the business.

"Caring Is a Powerful Business Advantage."

Scott Johnson

American Author

CHAPTER 6

IT'S ALL ABOUT THE CLIENT

I can't repeat this enough...the way you consistently treat your clients will determine the success of your business.

What served me well throughout my real estate career was my natural instinct to put myself in the shoes of the client. How would I feel in their position? How would I want to be treated? What would I want to know? How soon would I want to know it? Every step of the process I would be thinking of them and their position.

The longer you're in business, the more you have to remind yourself that your clients don't do this every day. Many real estate transactions are emotional for people who are going through tough life events – empty nester, estate sale for someone who lost a loved one, divorce, loss of job, or job transfer. We are not salespeople; we are counselors and educators. We educate throughout the process, giving them the information so they can make a smart decision. Give them their options, and let them decide. You can offer your professional advice, but ask their permission first. Don't just give it – they may not want it. I believe asking permission shows respect. I never had anyone say "No," but it could happen.

When you put yourself in your client's shoes, they will feel and see your empathy and compassion. When you feel their pain, they know; it will be obvious to them by your tone, your words, and your actions.

You can better serve your clients by asking tough questions and really listening to their answers. An example of a tough question: "Are you behind in your payments?" When the house is worth less than what they owe: "Do you have a way to get the $10,000 that you would need to bring to closing?" It is not easy to ask these questions, but the answers will help you better serve your client by getting the property sold. Another tough question, when you see the red flags: "Do you have a financial hardship?" If they do, they may qualify for a short sale. (A short sale is when a homeowner owes more than the house is worth, and the bank may be willing to accept less than what's owed.)

No matter where you are in your career, always stay humble. There is a fine line between confidence and arrogance. You can be both confident and humble. It's in the tone of your voice and in the words you choose. Know when something is difficult for someone to hear, and feel for them.

The age-old saying is that you never get a second chance to make a great first impression. It's still true. When you meet with a client for the first time, whether it's a buyer or a seller, you need to set expectations and explain every step of the process. Adversity happens when expectations differ. If what you describe is not agreeable to the client, the client will speak up. You can then both discuss the issue and decide if a more customized plan is needed.

What do most people want or expect from any industry? They want answers to their questions quickly. They want service immediately. They want to speak to a live person when they call. Most of the time when I call a business, I get voice mail, and I'm frustrated – or they transfer me to different departments, and I can be on hold for what feels like forever. I understand voice mail now and then, but it has become standard practice at many businesses, especially real estate.

You would expect that they would return calls promptly. But they don't. It can be days before calls are returned. And e-mails are just as bad, if not worse.

You should set your own standard for returning calls or e-mails. Our policy is for calls to be returned within three hours and e-mails within 24 hours. The real estate industry average for e-mail response is five days. There was an article in our trade publication regarding this issue and the fact that the real estate industry needs to improve the response time.

A CASE IN POINT:

One of our agents and our buyer were sitting at a closing when our buyer's phone rang. He answered and said, "No, I'm all set. In fact, I am sitting at the closing right now." He hung up and shared that he finally got a call back from the other agent he had called to inquire about the listing – 30 days earlier.

You also have to prepare your clients on how long it will take for you to respond to their call. Explain how long your appointments are typically. We advise our agents not to answer their cell phone when they are with a client. You need to focus on the one client you are with.

Other than being with a client, at a family event, in the shower, eating, sleeping, or sick, you should answer your phone. This is most likely an important life event for your client and should be your top priority.

If you're going to be unavailable for an extended length of time, you need to have someone cover for you. Agents typically get coverage when they go on vacation. Many of our agents still handle all negotiations even when they are on vacation. This is not typical, but it's one of the ways that we distinguish ourselves from our competitors. It also helps with another critical area – giving feedback.

Homesellers expect to get feedback from showings as soon as possible. Explain how your showing feedback works, and whatever you tell your client, be sure to keep your word. Don't overpromise and underdeliver.

Every year in Maine there are 23,000 properties on average that expire from the Multiple Listing Service. (For those of you who are not in the real estate industry, these are homes that were listed with an agent and failed to sell before the listing agreements expired, were withdrawn, or terminated.)

The most frequent complaint we hear is, "We never got feedback." Sometimes we hear, "Our feedback was vague." Some say, "We never heard anything" or "We never heard from our agent." Others were never notified that their listing agreement expired.

What's sad is if the agent would have taken the time and followed up with the feedback after showings, the home could have sold. The purpose of feedback is to figure out how to motivate the buyer or the buyer agent to try to produce a written offer. Make feedback one of your top priorities, and you and your seller will be on your way to a closing.

Our clients love the fact that they can speak to a live person when they call and usually they can get their questions answered right away.

SUCCESS STORY:

One of our agents was reviewing the feedback on one of his listings when he noticed a few positive comments about the house. They loved the house, but they thought the price was too high. Our agent called the buyer agent (from another company) and asked her why they were not writing an offer. He found out they did want to make an offer, but she had discouraged them because it was too low, and she didn't want to waste her time. The property was listed at $143,000 – they wanted to offer $125,000 with the seller paying the points/closing costs. The Fontaine agent said, "Just write it up, and I will present it."

She asked, "Do you think they'll take it?"

He answered, "I don't know, but let me present it; just write it up!"

She replied, "Just present it verbally."

He said, "It would be much better to get it in writing."

She refused. So our agent called the seller and explained the situation. The seller came back with $139,000 but would not pay points/closing costs. Our agent advised the seller to do a reverse offer and get it back to the potential buyer in writing. The seller agreed and signed the reverse offer, and it was immediately e-mailed to the buyer agent. The agent presented the reverse offer and the buyer countered (in writing) at $135,000 but still asked the seller to pay the $5,000 in points/closing costs. The seller countered in writing that he would accept the $135,000 but not pay the points/closing costs. The buyer signed the counter, and the property was under contract and closed successfully a month later.

What happens when agents don't get or give feedback or analyze the feedback? The house typically does not sell and becomes expired. No Sale.

This buyer agent would never have told our agent about the buyer wanting to make a low offer.

Let's not discourage buyers from writing offers. It's a starting point. None of us like to present low offers, but it's our fiduciary duty to present all offers. The seller could get upset, but we still need to do it. Share with your clients that they should not be insulted with a low offer. The buyers love the house enough to make an offer. Be insulted with all the buyers that looked at the house but didn't even make an offer. Explain that this is a process, and let's just go through the process one step at a time. This is a process.

Another reason why some homes may not have sold is they may have been crossed off the showing list.

It can be a huge problem trying to reach an agent to set up a showing if they don't have a system or a dedicated person who only handles showings 24/7.

It can be extremely frustrating for the buyer agent. Many times the calls are not returned. Weekends are the worst. So these homesellers don't even realize they missed showings. They don't realize that buyer agents will cross it off the list and intend to hopefully show it next time around. But what typically happens is the buyers find a home they love, and they never get to see the homes that had to be crossed off the list because they couldn't reach the listing agent.

Hopefully you will have a good system and not lose showing requests for your clients. Return all showing request calls promptly so you don't lose opportunities for your clients. Missed showings could be a missed sale.

ANOTHER SUCCESS STORY:

One of our agents received a call from a past buyer client who had just closed the previous day. His roof was leaking after a torrential rain, and he felt the seller should be responsible – he wanted help in paying for repairs.

Our agent called the listing agent, who refused to call his past client. His client was a friend, and he didn't want to get involved. Many agents rationalize by saying, "My job is done." Our job is never done if we want clients for life. Building relationships means helping out when you're needed. It's that simple.

Our agent proceeded to call the other agent's past client and explained the situation. The seller showed concern and agreed to meet at the property. Our agent, buyer, and seller met at the property the next day and were able to come to a resolution. The buyer paid for the materials, and the seller paid for the labor. Everyone was happy.

Six weeks later the other agent's past client (the seller) called our agent to purchase a $250,000 home. He was impressed with how our agent had taken care of the buyer. Now that he was a buyer, he wanted the same kind of service and after-the-sale care. He had been impressed with our agent and disappointed that his friend, the real estate agent, had not bothered to call him to tell him about the issue.

It's important to take care of your client after the sale (and after you have been paid). It's just the right thing to do. When things go bad, and your seller makes the wrong decision even though you advised him or her differently, both you and the seller learn a lesson from that mistake. You must share that story with your future clients so they can also learn from your experience. This can save your future clients a lot of heartache; they don't need to make the same mistakes. This is how you can make a difference. This is how you add value.

The most challenging part of my career was the first eight years. I was overwhelmed. Real estate is definitely not easy money. Unfortunately, the public thinks it is. You have to work hard, and you have a huge responsibility. A home purchase or sale is typically a person's largest investment and asset. We realize that it's our fiduciary duty to do right by our client. When an agent tries to do it all, things can easily fall through the cracks. When you start feeling guilty that you are shortchanging your clients, it's time to make some changes. When you make promises you can't keep, it's time to hire help.

I was never willing to sacrifice my family life for the business. I never missed a family event because I had a listing appointment on that special day. It was non-negotiable. I remember an agent telling me he had squeezed in an appointment and ended up missing an important family function. He told me he felt so guilty the whole time he was at the appointment that it was difficult for him to concentrate. It must have affected his listing presentation – he didn't get the listing, and he didn't get to enjoy his family making great memories. That was a hard lesson. He told me he would never let that happen again.

I believe I was a better agent for putting my family first, because when I was at my appointments, the people had my full attention. I was not preoccupied with what was going on with my family.

There does come a time when one person can't do it all. When your business grows, you need to grow with it. You are growing out of necessity.

Before I had buyer agents, I was giving away new buyer leads to agents in my office. I chose the agents wisely because I wanted to make sure they would take good care of them. I knew it would be a reflection on me. There was just not enough time to do it all.

A typical day would consist of finding new listings for current buyers by calling "For Sale by Owners" and "Expireds." Then I had to put up signs, take pictures, write ads, do listing paperwork, meet the appraiser at listings, check with the lender on the loan process, solve problems with pending sales, counsel my buyers and sellers, set up showings, call sellers with feedback after every showing, go to closings, etc.

It is impossible for one person to do it all and do it well. I tried for several years, and I couldn't do it. And that's why I started delegating by giving away some new buyer leads to agents who had more time to serve these people.

I should have started the team earlier, but there was no such thing as teams back then. I did what I thought was best at the time. All that I know is that I needed help. When I did start hiring help, I didn't even realize I was beginning to build a team until I went to the Craig Proctor seminar. I heard comments from homeowners that agents would say, "If you list with Brenda, you'll never hear from her." They didn't understand the team concept. I was actually giving more personal service than ever. They just didn't understand that because of the team system, I actually had more time to spend on advising and counseling, and solving problems because all the other stuff was being handled by a licensed support staff, and the personal service was improving by leaps and bounds.

The licensed support staff takes care of all the behind-the-scene details typically handled by the listing agent. This gives the listing agent the opportunity to counsel and advise the seller/buyer clients. The listing agent has time to analyze the feedback, discuss it with the seller, and listen carefully to the client. Listing agents have time to keep a pulse on the ever-changing market in order to better counsel the sellers. They also concentrate on "producing" offers on their listings and attend closings. Everything else is handled by the support staff.

I know, I know – you're probably getting tired of me saying this. But… treat your clients like family. If your mom were selling her home, how would you want her to be treated? How would you want one of her largest assets to be protected? Put the clients' needs and best interest before your own. Communicate. Give them updates throughout the process. Be responsive. Return calls promptly. Educate them by sharing your knowledge and experience. Share your success stories. Share the challenging transactions you were able to save and share how you got to the closing table. You can add tremendous value by preparing them for each step of the process. No one likes surprises. Put yourself in their shoes. What would you expect? And then exceed expectations. Always keep your word. Trust is the foundation of client loyalty.

If you make a mistake, admit it. Apologize. And then make it right. If you make a mistake that costs the client money, you need to step up to the plate. If it means you have to pay for your mistake, just do it. It's all about the client. The client is always right. Don't argue with a client. It's a no-win situation. You need to make yourself available. Real estate is not a 9-5 job. You are always on call. Our company is always open. We have licensed staff on call after business hours. Take good care of your clients, and they'll take good care of you.

That's why we make strategic, thoughtful decisions when adding a member to the team. The first thing we look for in a team member is a positive attitude. You can't train "nice." We have done well in finding team members who love helping people and who share the same values. We look for counselors and advisor type personalities, not high-pressure salespeople. No one wants to be pressured. The client is the decision maker. We are there for our clients: to educate them, give options, and then let them decide – just like homeowners who want to know what their home is worth. We share the info, give them their options, and they choose the list price. If it is outside the realm of reality, that opinion is definitely shared. You must have the courage to tell them the truth; otherwise, it's a major disservice. So our future team members must agree with this philosophy.

On the buyer side, our team goal is to find the right house for the client, not just any house. And the future team member must be a team player and honor our team mission, and again share in our family values of honesty and integrity.

One of the questions I usually ask someone I'm interviewing is how they would deal with an irate client. We deal with so many emotional clients; they have "ups" and "downs." We can do everything perfectly, but things can still get stressful because things can change quickly in real estate. We need to listen carefully, and stay calm because they will calm down too. If we get as stressed out as they are, we are not helping them. Ask them what they want or feel they need to rectify the issue, and let's do what we can to make it right.

There is nothing more stressful than giving your client bad news. We all hate to disappoint our clients, but there are things that are out of our control. Sometimes the unexpected happens.

CASE IN POINT:

One day I had to make that kind of call to one of my repeat clients, Mr. & Mrs. B. The closing had been delayed – we wouldn't be closing the following day. I called and spoke with Mr. B and broke the news. Closing day now needed to be postponed until further notice. Mr. B. was fine and just said to call him when it was rescheduled.

But then I received a call from Mrs. B. She was totally distraught. She was yelling at the top of her lungs. I tried to calm her down by remaining calm and letting her know that I was on top of it, and I would do everything I could to move it along. I told her I would be staying in constant touch with appropriate parties.

There was nothing I could do or say; she was upset, and she hung up on me. These people had been my clients for several years, and we had developed a great relationship. This was going to be the third closing with them. So I cried and cried. I would cry, then I would stop. Then I would think of what had just happened, and I'd start crying all over again. This went on for a couple of hours and I developed a terrible migraine. Then the phone rang and it was Mrs. B. And she said, "Brenda, I am so sorry. I don't know what came over me. I know it's not your fault. I should not blame you. This 100-degree weather is really getting to me. Just let us know when the closing will be rescheduled." I said, "Absolutely, I will. I appreciate your call."

And I did appreciate her call to apologize. I should not have let it affect me the way it did. It is so easy to take things personally. Clients are upset with the situation, not us. She was frustrated moving in 100-degree weather, and the call just intensified her frustration. The agent is always the first person on the front lines to get their first reaction. You need to prepare to stay professional and stay calm. This happened during my first five years in the business. I knew if I wanted to last in this business, I had to control my emotions.

I am still sensitive and still emotional at times, but I never cried again as much as I did that day.

We did close a few days later, and they continued to work with me. Their adult children became great clients too.

World-class service also means making clients feel comfortable and at peace with their decision to hire you. It's extremely important to offer guarantees to get them to that comfort level. Consider offering a cancellation guarantee. If the client is not happy with your service, they can obtain a release from their contract. It's solidifying your commitment that you will be on your toes at all times because they can fire you if you don't hold your end of the bargain. It's a risk-free agreement for them. This is how you raise the bar and maintain world-class service. They know that they can fire you if you don't do what you say you're going to do.

That means being diligent in getting feedback on every showing, and communicating it back to the client as soon as possible. And respond to showing requests quickly so the seller doesn't miss out on a showing. It means communicating any signs of possible interest.

How do you know if your clients are happy? You ask them to fill out a client survey questionnaire. The only way you can continue to give world-class service is to monitor your service. Mail or e-mail surveys after each and every closing.

The agent should explain to the client how important the feedback is. And when they know it's important to you to get it back, the clients are very receptive to get it done. We also tell them we want both negative and positive feedback.

We have tons of surveys that we send out, and we get tons back. We read them at our weekly team meetings (another great way to recognize the agents and praise them for a job well done). We also post them on social media. The agents love the recognition, and everyone loves to hear the feedback.

We aspire to be the best, not the biggest. The largest real estate company doesn't mean the best real estate company. The best real estate agent, team, or company is the one that provides the best client care. The best client care will bring the best results for its clients. When you want the best burger, do you go to the biggest hamburger chain? Or do you go to the local restaurant that offers the best quality burger, the best service, and the best experience?

You will build a successful business because of client loyalty that lasts a lifetime. You may fear to make a change. How do you know when it's the right time to move to the next level?

Whether it's changing real estate companies, changing teams, or starting a team, there are signs to look for.

Are you so busy that you're feeling overwhelmed? Are you starting to feel like you're short-changing your clients? Are you making promises that you're not able to keep? Are you feeling guilty?

You're not going to be able to create clients for life unless you get help. Maybe you need administrative support. If you already have the administrative support but it's still too much to handle, you need a buyer agent. Hire that buyer agent. Just be sure to do your due diligence. Does this person return calls promptly? Do you have the same core values?

Do you see yourself as a team member/team player? Interview with different teams to see which one is the right fit for you. There is no limit to what you can accomplish. Nothing can happen until you take action.

Are you ready for the next level?

TOP FIVE LESSONS LEARNED FROM CREATING INCREDIBLE CLIENT RELATIONSHIPS:

1. Put yourself in the shoes of your clients to better understand their circumstances.

2. Communicate and educate your client on every step of the process.

3. Keep your word!

4. Do the right thing, even if it means you don't make the sale.

5. Creating amazing client relationships guarantees success.

"I Wonder if Fears Ever Really Go Away, or if They Just Lose Their Power over Us."

Veronica Roth

American Novelist and Best-Selling Author
Allegiant, Divergents #3

CHAPTER 7

REFLECTIONS

I have had an amazing life considering that I never expected to reach adulthood. I would lie in bed at night, praying and begging God to allow me to reach my thirteenth birthday. After reaching that milestone, I would ask God to allow me to experience having a boyfriend, then came the prayer for marriage and children. I then asked God to allow me to watch my children grow up. Today, I pray and ask God to allow me the opportunity to dance at my grandchildren's weddings.

Most people will tell you that the older they get, the more they appreciate life. I have always appreciated life. I have always appreciated each and every moment because I have always known that life can be taken away in a millisecond. My mother told me so, and I believed everything she said.

Before I would head out the door to go outside and play or leave for school, my mom would say, "Come give me a kiss goodbye. This could be the last time you ever see me. You never know when something bad can happen." So I grew up fearing something bad could happen. Most people think bad things only happen to other people.

So I would give her a kiss goodbye and say a silent prayer, begging God not to let anything bad happen to her. I lived my life always in fear of something bad happening to us, but on the other hand, I actually appreciated each stage of my life. I grew up knowing that my life was a gift not to be taken for granted, and appreciated each and every day.

When my mom was sober, she could be a good, loving and caring mom. She was proud of my accomplishments. When she drank, though, she was possessed by the devil. She was mean, self-centered and verbally, physically, and mentally abusive. The worst was when she would threaten to kill me. She threatened me as a teenager and also after I was married.

When I was a teenager, she actually showed up in my bedroom one night, after we had an argument about my boyfriend. I was lying in bed just staring at the ceiling, in deep thought, and she just walked in waving a kitchen knife in my face, with the look of evil and hatred in her eyes. Is it possible that she was just trying to scare me? Maybe. But I wasn't taking any chances, and I locked my bedroom door after that night.

Looking back, I believe if she really wanted to kill me, she would have, but that night still haunts me with recurring nightmares.

Even when she was sober, she could be very cruel, especially when she was nursing a hangover. She would go into very deep depressions, staying in bed for days. However, she did mellow out and stop drinking when she was in her late fifties. Unfortunately, she was never able to conquer the depression.

I vowed that if I would be blessed with children, I would not worry them needlessly. My mom taught me so much about what not to do.

My mom ruined many family vacations because of her "silent treatments." I saw how much valuable time was wasted by using her "silent treatment" on me and my dad. It was especially difficult on vacations. As an adult, I chose not to go on trips with her because of this. She didn't realize that every time she used that "silent treatment" as punishment, she was also punishing herself.

How long do you stay upset with a family member, friend, or co-worker when you have a disagreement? Time is passing by, and you can never get it back. Choose the high road and forgive and move on. Don't lose that time to silence. You could be making wonderful memories.

Fortunately, there was an occasion that allowed me to realize that I was not my mother.

One day she showed me her wrinkled 65-year-old hands and said, "Look how old I am getting, Brenda." I stared at her hands and looked up into her large hazel eyes. She looked so sad. There was that look of depression again. I said nothing. I knew that it would not matter. Nothing I had ever said or done had helped get her out of that deep hole of depression that she had dug herself into decades earlier.

One morning recently, I looked in the mirror and saw a resemblance of my mom staring back at me. I always thought I looked like my dad, and I always wanted to be like my dad. I clung to the belief that I looked like him and that I had his demeanor and his ethics. He was trustworthy, a people pleaser, and a hard worker. He was my hero and my role model, and my mom always pointed out that I was my father's daughter – the spitting image in every way, including the dark brown eyes and the dark brown hair.

So the day I saw my mother's reflection in the bathroom mirror was a terrible shock. It seemed to just happen overnight – one morning I had aged twenty years and my mother crept out. It scared the hell out of me. If I resemble my mom this much, how much of her actually rubbed off on me? My mom was a depressed alcoholic most of her life. She suffered from mental illness according to the psychiatrist she visited every month at Tri-County Mental Health.

I realize that I have always been fearful of being just like her. I have a long list of fears: flying, public speaking, death, illness of myself and my family. I have overcome many of my fears by working through them. You have to have the courage to move on and do it anyway. Courage is not absence of fear. It's doing it anyway until it gets easier as time goes on, as Susan Jeffers says in her book *Feel the Fear and Do It Anyway.* My love of reading has helped me tremendously.

I do struggle with my "skeletons in the closet." I hope, though, to have learned from my mom's mistakes. I must see her mistakes as lessons she taught me. I believe my mom's flaws are the greatest gifts she could ever have given me. I wouldn't be the person I am today without having lived through these adversities. How about you? Have you been through adversities that have shaped your life? Are you choosing the high road and choosing to become a victor or a victim? My mother did not speak to her sister (her only sibling) for over 20 years. They did reunite later in life and became very close again, but how sad that they lost all that time. Another lesson learned from my mom: We can all learn from other people's mistakes.

I have had a great life, and I thank God every day for my blessings. I surround myself with positive people. I read daily affirmations and positive quotes to be reminded to be grateful every single day. Even when you have a bad day, look for the one positive moment of the day and focus on that.

I do have my moments of negative thoughts. I do struggle some days, but I never give up the fight. Some days are more difficult than others. These days you just have to focus on the good in your life and know that the struggle you are going through right now is temporary. Life doesn't have to be perfect to be good.

I loved my mom; I miss her every day, and I know she did the best she could. I like to remember her good days. My treasured moments were when she would tell me she loved me, how proud she was of me, and how I could be whatever I wanted to be in life.

I got to a point in my life that I knew I had to forgive my mom for the bad times and embrace the good times for my own mental health. I knew I had to let go of all the childhood baggage to move forward, so I focused on the good she did. You can't be a victim forever. Victims fail in life; victors are successful. So I decided to be grateful for the adversities in my life. It made me who I am. And it's because of the sum total of the good and bad that I had the burning desire to succeed. Failure would not be an option for me!

Don't let failure be an option for you! But you must not be afraid to fail. You will experience failures before you reach success.

The year before my mom passed away, she became very ill and was admitted to the ICU. She was in and out of consciousness for days. When she finally stabilized and became coherent, she shocked me with the first words that came out of her mouth and with fear in her eyes. She said, "Brenda, I know I haven't been a good mother. I know I did some bad things. I know it was wrong. Can you forgive me? I love you, I need you to forgive me. I'm so sorry." With my eyes filling up with tears, I said, "Of course, I forgive you. I love you, too." I am so grateful for that moment. She lived another 16 months. Our relationship was much better. My mother had come out of that semi-coma a changed woman. Never in my life had I ever heard her apologize to me or to anyone. She had never admitted to any wrongdoing. This was completely out of character. I had just witnessed a miracle.

I had just been given a precious gift. Little did she know I had decided to forgive her decades earlier.

I choose not to hold grudges; I choose to forgive. It's better for my health. Do you need to forgive someone? Or do you need to ask for forgiveness? Saying the words, "I'm sorry" can save so much time apart from those you love. Even if you have nothing to be sorry about, those two little words can make your life so much happier. So take the high road. It's so worth it. It's so liberating! Don't let this baggage get in the way of your happiness.

I choose to take the high road, and I live each day in the moment while I continue to plan for an outstanding future.

My husband and my children have been a great source of joy and strength for me. I am proud that our children will continue our family business with the same family values, the same work ethic, honesty, and integrity that my dad passed on to me.

Our daughters know we believe in them. They know we are their #1 fans and have been since they were born. We are so proud of each and every one of our children. When I speak of our children, I am referring to my three daughters and my three sons-in-law. They are all our children and we love them all very much. I believe there are no accidents and no coincidences and that everything happens for a reason. Every adversity is a blessing in disguise.

Failure would not be an option for me. Don't let failure be an option for you. You must not be afraid to fail. You will experience failure before reaching success. You must fail your way to success.

Don't be afraid to dream big. Big dreams do come true. If someone like me can do it, you can reach your goal and realize your dream too. You just have to take that first baby step to the next level of your journey. Baby steps are easier. And they are better than not doing anything at all. Slow and steady is better.

My hope for you is that you can dig deep to get the courage you need to take that baby step outside your comfort zone. Why be ordinary when you can be extraordinary with just a little extra effort?

It's a good life. Everyone has the same opportunities; not everyone chooses to take action to make things happen. And those that choose to take the action reach success. Keep learning, stay positive, and never give up; you will be on your way to reaching your goals and making your dreams come true. And believe that there is no limit to what you can accomplish. It's all up to you! Don't let self-limiting beliefs stop you from achieving your goals. I know it's not easy, but I am proof that you can do it. I could have allowed my mom's fears to impose limits on me. As I grew my real estate business, I refused to allow my fears to limit my future – I knew if I did, it would limit the future of my children and grandchildren.

You can take action too, in spite of your fear. Don't see challenges as problems; see them as opportunities. It will change your future.

It's a very good life, and I believe there is a lot more good life to live for me and for you.

"If you can dream it, then you can achieve it. You will get all you want in life if you help enough people get what they want."
– Zig Ziglar

FIVE LESSONS LEARNED FROM ADVERSITY

1. There are lessons to be learned from negative situations.

2. You get to choose who you wish to be... it's not up to anyone else.

3. Courage isn't the absence of fear; it's moving forward in the face of it.

4. Don't be afraid to fail.

5. Dream big dreams AND take action to accomplish them.

"Keep a Diary of Your Daily Wins and Accomplishments. If Your Life Is Worth Living, It's Worth Recording."

Marilyn Grey

Author

"If You Are Working on Something Exciting that You Really Care About, You Don't Have to Be Pushed. The Vision Pulls You."

Steve Jobs

Apple Founder

FINAL THOUGHTS

The choice I made to close my daycare business and get into real estate full-time was a huge leap of faith. I didn't have all the answers, but I still jumped in with blind faith. I believed it could be a life changer, and I knew it was up to me to make it happen. I knew I had a huge responsibility, and I also knew that my husband would support me and be there for me every step of the way. I am so proud of what we have accomplished. There is no way I could have ever accomplished this alone. It was definitely a team effort.

Looking back, I am still amazed how everything fell into place like pieces of a puzzle. I do believe it was God's plan, and it was all meant to be. I always knew in my heart that I wanted to help others. I thought of nursing, but there was no money for college. And then my husband planted the seed about a real estate career. Who would have ever thought that my real estate career would lead to a successful family business? God knew.

Who would have ever thought that I could write a book? Or would? It was something I wanted to do but had no idea I could actually do it.

Brian Buffini inspired me when he told us all at a MasterMind Summit that each one of us had a story to tell. He encouraged everyone to just do it. Brian and his team clearly live their mission of impacting and improving the lives of others. He definitely impacted and improved my life. And I will be forever grateful.

Many people comment on how lucky we are. They tell us that our success is due to the fact that we are a family business. I do agree that it's one of the reasons, but not the sole reason.

There have been challenges, as I mentioned before, and we worked through them. We set boundaries and created rules. A family business does have a huge advantage because of the trust we have amongst each other, the family pride, the commitment to its success, and the shared family values. And the positive and energized environment spreads through the team. That's why there are so many successful family businesses.

My husband and I are very proud of the role our children have played and continue to play in the success of the business. We couldn't ask for more commitment and dedication. We are also proud of our powerhouse team. Our team members are the best of the best in the business. They are committed to exceeding expectations and dedicated to keep living the team mission day in and day out. And we couldn't ask for a better licensed support staff – average experience for each individual is 12+ years, with 88 years of combined experience. And they are the backbone of our team.

I wrote this book to fulfill my promise to God – to share my knowledge and experience to help others be successful. I hope you were able to relate to the 16 personal stories throughout the book, or maybe you're a new agent and you have learned from the stories.

This book should be the beginning of a relationship. I would like nothing more than to hear from you on how it impacted your life.

How can I further help you with your dreams or aspirations? Have you been motivated to start your own business? Or are you a real estate agent and you've decided to take the next step to either hire your first assistant or your first buyer agent? Maybe you have already shown courage in the face of fear? Wherever you are in your journey, I would love to hear your story.

My hope for you is that you, too, can gather up the courage to push through the fear rather than be limited by the fear, and you can begin your limitless journey.

BRENDA'S SUCCESS TIPS

1. **Be a risk taker**. There is no gain without risk. You can't achieve success without having the courage to not let fear control your life. If you wait for the fear to disappear, you will be waiting for a long time. So just do it!

2. **You are the CEO of your real estate business even if you are not the broker-owner.** You must take charge and take responsibility. Too many agents see themselves as employees. Show up to work every day. Be proactive. Set goals (daily, weekly, monthly, and yearly).

3. **Establish daily minimum standards**. Be disciplined and committed so you don't lose momentum. It's a lot easier to keep going than it is to play catch-up. If you don't have 2-3 hours to make prospecting calls, then just make five contacts that day. Do something. Something is better than nothing.

4. **Be a lifelong learner.** Read daily, even if it's just 15 minutes. Watch webinars, listen to podcasts, and go to events. Invest a minimum of one hour a week on your education. It will put you far in front of the pack of those who only do what's required.

5. **Care about your clients.** Listen 80% of the time and speak 20 % of the time. Ask tough questions so you have a

better understanding of their situation so you can find a solution to their problem. A good communicator asks a lot of questions and is a good problem solver. Great problem solvers became great agents. When you continue caring after the sale, you create lifelong relationships. Our agents continue to hone their skills by sharing their challenges weekly with the other top-notch agents on our team. By sharing and brainstorming, everyone learns to focus on the solution rather than the problem. We have the best brainstorming sessions at our weekly team meetings. Even veterans of 20+ years learn from these sessions. And since everyone is willing to share, our clients benefit because another seller has a successful, stress-free closing and another buyer is able to purchase the home of their dreams.

6. **Be honest.** Have the guts to be honest even when it's hard, and even though you know you will disappoint. You must do the right thing.

I got a call one spring day from a repeat client. The husband had decided to take a job offer and they were ready to put their home on the market. I had been there six months earlier sharing comparable sales in the $350,000-$425,000 range. We all had agreed that $400,000 was a fair price. Now I had to break the bad news that nothing had sold in Lewiston or Auburn over $400,000 since our last meeting. The highest sale in the previous six months sold for $376,000 (and it was our listing and sale). Everything else had sold for less.

Now, the tough part – I had to disappoint them. I love real estate, but I hate sharing bad news with sellers. Sellers hate hearing that their home is worth less than they think, but I know it's in their best interest to know the truth. This is when it takes guts.

So I shared the most recent sales and shared my professional opinion: They should put it on the market for $375,000. They were devastated. Their first response was, "Let's price it at $400,000, but we would listen to an offer." I told them we could do that if that was their decision, but that they should seriously reconsider. I explained how much more informed buyers are than ever before because of the internet. Buyers would immediately know it was overpriced, and they would quickly eliminate it as even a possibility. And based on the market data, there had been zero buyers in the $400,000 range in the previous six months. They argued that by pricing it at $375,000 they would have no room to negotiate. I responded with, "I would rather you have offers to refuse than no offers at all."

They agreed to list it at $375,000. We had a $360,000 offer two weeks later. The sellers countered at $374,500. The buyers came back at $370,000. The sellers' final counter was $373,500. The buyers accepted. We closed 30 days later, and my clients were extremely happy.

What if I had just listed it at $400,000 without giving them the market overview? It would have most likely stayed on the market for months, maybe even a year. And the chances of getting even $375,000 would have been lost. Buyers always want to know how long a house has been on the market. And when it's been a while, they're more apt to make lowball offers.

7. **Fail your way to success.** Remember, the more "No" responses you get, the closer you are to a "Yes." Don't be the one that quits because you don't realize how close you are to success. Don't give up. Don't blame others for your failures. Ask yourself, "What could I have done differently?"

8. **Be an educator, advisor, and counselor.** Educate your clients on the process, give them their options, share your professional opinion, then let them decide.

9. **Have a balanced life.** Make a work-life balance a priority. Keep your priorities straight. You can have a successful career and still have a personal life. Put your family time and personal time in your calendar first. Enjoy a personal life because you can never get that time back. Which is more valuable? Time or money? Lose them both and which one can you get back? Imagine all the success you want but no one to share it with? For me, that success would be worthless.

10. **Have fun at work.** We have so much fun! Team members are our extended family. We share personal stories. We find reasons to celebrate, to appreciate and to recognize. Life is too short not to enjoy your co-workers and make your workplace a happy place.

11. **Keep your word.** Don't overpromise and underdeliver. You must underpromise and overdeliver. When you tell your client you will be calling them back by Thursday, call them back Wednesday afternoon. You build trust by keeping your word, and trust creates loyalty. And loyalty creates clients for life.

When you earn the trust and respect of your clients by giving them the world-class service they deserve, they will be inspired to share their experience with their family and friends. And there is no better marketing than word of mouth.

BRENDA'S TOP DISTINCTIONS OF A SUPERSTAR SALES PROFESSIONAL

- Treating it like a real job
- Always start early
- Proactive (prospecting for buyers and sellers)
- Positive mindset
- Willing to learn and continue to learn forever to be highly skilled
- Strong work ethic
- Committed
- Caring
- Client focused
- Trustworthy
- Good follow-up
- Good listeners
- Servant's heart
- Knowing the importance of creating a relationship for life
- Problem-solving skills

BRENDA'S FAMILY BUSINESS RULES

1. Agree to disagree.

2. Be open to new ideas (everyone).

3. Don't stay upset or angry for more than five minutes – then get over it (works in a marriage too).

4. Don't talk business at family gatherings.

5. Understand the importance of open communication; no one should be afraid to speak up and tell it like it is.

6. Keep your personal life and business life separate. Your spouse doesn't need to know every detail to every transaction. Don't take them along the roller coaster ride. You're spreading more stress. Besides, unless you both represent the client, it's illegal. It's against your fiduciary duties.

7. Before you hire or recruit a family member or friend, consider his/her previous career. Was it something in the service industry – teacher, police officer, firefighter, sales, etc.? I believe the best agents were already experienced in servicing clients/customers. They already have the human relations skills necessary to be outstanding in real estate.

   Our two sons-in-law and three daughters had all been involved in customer service. (Crystal had worked as a teenager at a store selling sports equipment, helping customers with their needs.) I believe it's definitely a huge factor in becoming successful.

You need to look for people who love to be around other people, the personality type that has a servant's heart who really cares about people and wants to genuinely help them. That is what makes a great REALTOR®.

Dear Reader,

We would consider it a privilege to have the opportunity to serve you in your real estate needs.

The Fontaine Family is a highly skilled real estate team of effective negotiators and problem solvers dedicated to making your real estate goals a reality. Fontaine is a family-owned, full-service, real estate boutique brokerage with a long-standing tradition of excellence, professionalism, and integrity. We have maintained successful business relationships since 1983.

We specialize in residential as well as commercial properties. We also have a short sale and REO department. In addition, we offer turnkey new construction packages (no construction loan needed).

We are ready to help you with your real estate needs in Maine and look forward to helping you make a smart and informed decision.

Visit **brendafontaine.com**

THE FONTAINE DIFFERENCE

F ontaine clients receive the greatest possible attention and focus because of the systemized approach the team system provides.   Each of our real estate professionals has the support of the licensed support staff:

- Personal coaching by Brenda, Bill, and Clay
- Mentoring by the top 1% in the nation
- Listing Manager
- Field Coordinator
- Showing Feedback Coordinator
- Lead Manager/REO Specialist
- Closing Coordinator/Short Sale Specialist
- Marketing Director/Trainer

FONTAINE
BUSINESS MODEL

Most agents spend 20% of their career with a client, 80% doing other things.

If you can reverse that and spend 80% with clients and 20% doing other things, you can work half as many hours and make 3 times the money – <u>net</u>. It's not about your gross income; it's about your net income.

The Fontaine team believes in serving more clients with world-class service, while living a well-balanced life.

Should you trade your time for money or your money for more time? It's your choice. Time is precious and in short supply. You can always make more money, but you can't make more time.

Do you have a Maine referral? We would love to help them. Whether they are buying or selling, you can rest assured that our family team will give them the care and attention they deserve. E-mail me:

limitless@fontaineteam.com

If you live in Maine, maybe you're interested in joining the Fontaine Team. We are not always hiring, but we are always looking for talent. Don't hesitate to reach out to me.

limitless@fontaineteam.com

WE WELCOME YOU TO JOIN OUR SOCIAL MEDIA COMMUNITY:

- Facebook   facebook.com/fontaineteam
- YouTube   youtube.com/fontaineteam
- Instagram   instagram.com/fontainehomes
- Twitter   twitter.com/fmlytm
- LinkedIn   linkedin.com/in/brendafontaine
- Pinterest   pinterest.com/fontaineteam

ABOUT THE AUTHOR

B renda Fontaine began her sales career at the age of 14 when she helped her mother sell Avon products by knocking on doors searching for customers.

In 1983 she became a real estate agent and knew instantly that she had found her passion. At the end of her second year, she started receiving top honors not only across the state, but also across the nation. She earned "Top All Around Agent" repeatedly, which is one of the most prestigious national awards earned by the ERA national franchise.

Today, Fontaine is CEO and broker/owner of Fontaine Family – The Real Estate Leader, which is consistently ranked one of the top agencies among the 1,001 Maine real estate companies.

Fontaine Family Team has been named repeatedly among the top 1,000 real estate professional teams in the United States by Real Trends as published in *The Wall Street Journal*.

Fontaine has closed over 6,000 transactions and nearly one billion dollars in sales volume since 1983.

Brenda keeps "family" in the Fontaine Family Team, where her three daughters, two sons-in-law, and husband are part of the growing business with locations in Auburn, Maine and Scarborough, Maine.

**BRENDA FONTAINE
OVER
$3,000,000**

1983

1995

1999

2001

2013

2016

2016

2016

Made in the USA
Columbia, SC
20 June 2023

18466053R00089